S. Hrg. 113–459

AUTHORIZATION FOR USE OF MILITARY FORCE AFTER IRAQ AND AFGHANISTAN

HEARING

BEFORE THE

COMMITTEE ON FOREIGN RELATIONS UNITED STATES SENATE

ONE HUNDRED THIRTEENTH CONGRESS

SECOND SESSION

MAY 21, 2014

Printed for the use of the Committee on Foreign Relations

Available via the World Wide Web: http://www.gpo.gov/fdsys/

U.S. GOVERNMENT PRINTING OFFICE

91–139 PDF   WASHINGTON : 2014

For sale by the Superintendent of Documents, U.S. Government Printing Office
Internet: bookstore.gpo.gov   Phone: toll free (866) 512–1800; DC area (202) 512–1800
Fax: (202) 512–2104   Mail: Stop IDCC, Washington, DC 20402–0001

(II)

CONTENTS

AUTHORIZATION FOR USE OF MILITARY FORCE AFTER IRAQ AND AFGHANISTAN

WEDNESDAY, MAY 21, 2014

U.S. SENATE,
COMMITTEE ON FOREIGN RELATIONS,
Washington, DC.

The committee met, pursuant to notice, at 10:03 a.m., in room SD–419, Dirksen Senate Office Building, Hon. Robert Menendez (chairman of the committee) presiding.

Present: Senators Menendez, Durbin, Murphy, Kaine, Markey, Corker, Rubio, Johnson, Flake, and McCain.

OPENING STATEMENT OF HON. ROBERT MENENDEZ, U.S. SENATOR FROM NEW JERSEY

The CHAIRMAN. Good morning. This hearing will come to order.

Let me welcome our panelists to this important hearing on how, when, and where the United States brings to bear the power of our military.

The 9/11 AUMF has served the United States well. It has provided broad authority for the United States to pursue and dismantle al-Qaeda in Afghanistan and Pakistan, and a foundation to authorize U.S. operations against al-Qaeda elsewhere, and against groups and individuals which have operationally associated themselves with al-Qaeda, like Al Qaeda in the Arabian Peninsula—an expansion that the Congress and U.S. courts have endorsed.

That said, with the winding down of significant U.S. military activities in Afghanistan by the end of this year, it is appropriate to begin reassessing the 9/11 AUMF, in light of new circumstances and new threats that have evolved over time. The President himself recognized this, a year ago, when he said that he looked forward to engaging Congress and the American people in efforts to refine and ultimately repeal the AUMF's mandate. He also said that he, "would not sign laws designed to expand this mandate further." I feel it is time to seriously consider what options and tools we have to counter what appears to be a continued, and, in some regions, growing, threat of terrorism to the United States. This hearing will consider existing authorities under the current authorization for the use of military force, as well as what additional statutory authorities may be required to confront ongoing threats associated with al-Qaeda and other terrorist entities that threaten the United States, as well as the President's inherent authorities.

I want to hear from our administration witnesses what the thinking has been in the executive branch about the current AUMF and options to either amend or develop a new AUMF to confront the changing threat environment.

I would ask all our witnesses to answer a simple question today. Is the 9/11 AUMF broken in some way? Is it obsolete? Is it inadequate to the threats we and our friends and allies face today and for the foreseeable future? If we amend or draft a new AUMF, what would this new authority look like? How would we determine which threats to pursue in order to secure ourselves at home and abroad?

And finally, I would like to hear the views of each of our witnesses on the prospect of repealing the Iraq AUMF, which I personally believe must be repealed. It is my understanding that, from a legal and operational perspective, there are no barriers to repeal and no deficiencies of needed authorities to assist the Government of Iraq in counterterrorism activities.

These are important questions that must be answered. Now, not at a moment of crisis, is a time to have this important dialogue. There is no issue more important to our national security than whether to use military force. And there is no other committee in the Senate that is seized with this issue more squarely than the Senate Foreign Relations Committee. Current and future threats necessitate our engagement and our attention.

So, with our thanks to the witnesses again for what I look forward to be an informative exchange, let me—before I turn to Senator Corker, we have received a statement, for the record, from Human Rights First on the issues we will cover in this hearing. I ask unanimous consent that it be included in the record. Without objection, so ordered.

The CHAIRMAN. Let me recognize the distinguished ranking member, Senator Corker, for his remarks.

OPENING STATEMENT OF HON. BOB CORKER, U.S. SENATOR FROM TENNESSEE

Senator CORKER. Mr. Chairman, I want to thank you for having this hearing.

And I want to thank the witnesses for taking their time to be here before us today and help us. And I want to thank you on two fronts. Number one, I know we have talked about this for some time, and you have honored a commitment, which I greatly appreciate, actually to people on both sides of the aisle. And I appreciate the way you have allowed there to be appropriate debate on this committee.

I know we both attended a sort of a discussion last night, that I found to be one of the most bizarre I have attended on Foreign Relations, on foreign policy in our country. And I am convinced more than ever that this discussion regarding the AUMF is an important place for us to weigh in and to help shape policy.

And I want to say, on the onset, that, to me, this is not about trying to limit the President in his abilities to carry out activities, that I think both of us consider to be very, very important to our security. It is more about us weighing in and actually giving the President the authorities he needs, but, at the same time, us having the responsibility to ensure that we have appropriate policies, especially with where we are today relative to terrorism around the world.

So, with that, I am going to read—I hate to read opening statements, but I am going to do that anyway. And again, I want to thank you for allowing us to weigh in on one of the most critical issues facing our country.

My hope is the committee can lead Congress to fulfilling its constitutional responsibilities on foreign policy and ensure that we, as a nation, pursue our national defense in a lawful and accountable way.

One week after the 9/11 attacks, Congress authorized the President to use all necessary and appropriate force against those nations, organizations, or persons he determined planned, authorized, committed, or aided the terrorist attacks that occurred on September the 11th, 2001. More than 12 years later, the President continues to rely on this same 60-word authorization to fight terrorist organizations around the world.

I understand why people are concerned and may think that seeking appropriate legal authorization for counterterrorism is either a way to seek expansion of war or attempt to restrict the President. From my perspective, neither is the case.

In the 13 years since the original authorization, the threat to our security has changed substantially. Today's threat is no longer about the hunt for bin Laden and those responsible for the 9/11 attacks. Today's threat is about affiliated groups metastasizing across the globe, and the current authorization simply does not make sense anymore. These evolving threats are not secret, and they are clearly openly recognized by this administration

A State Department report released in April said that, while al-Qaeda's central leadership is diminished, their affiliated groups are expanding, contributing to a 43-percent increase in global terrorist attacks in 2013 alone. The Chairman of the Joint Chiefs, Martin Dempsey, recently testified that the terrorists responsible for killing four Americans in Benghazi are not covered under the current AUMF. Perhaps the most problematic and ironic is the fact that the President may not have the authority to target the most ruthless terrorist organization in Syria, the Islamic State of Iraq and Syria, or ISIS, because of its split with al-Qaeda.

It would be easier for us to ignore these difficult issues or to buy the fantasy that al-Qaeda is dead or dying and that the tides of war are receding. But no serious observer can look to the world today without concluding that, for the foreseeable future, terrorist groups with global reach will continue to threaten our country, regardless of their link to the 9/11 attacks.

Rather than abdicating the responsibility for confronting this threat and leaving it to the executive branch, Congress has a responsibility to both provide the President with the legal authorities needed to ensure our security and to define the legal parameters in which this shall be pursued. This hearing provides members of this committee the opportunity to begin that process.

However, since the President suggested, in a May 2013 memo, that he would engage with Congress on this issue, he has been silent and done nothing. I believe this committee can and will act responsibly. I believe we can move forward in a bipartisan fashion to ensure that the law reflects reality, that counterterrorism operations respect the law, and that the President has the authority that he needs to keep America safe while respecting the Constitution.

This hearing is a first step in that direction. The bottom line is that an issue this critical to our security and liberty demands a robust and thorough debate from the elected officials of the American people. As difficult as it may be, Congress has to step up to the plate. It is our duty to have this debate. We cannot ask Americans to serve their country and risk their lives in the ongoing fight against terrorism if we will not take our responsibility seriously here.

So, with that, Mr. Chairman, thank you again for this great hearing, and I hope we will have some results after this hearing is concluded.

The CHAIRMAN. Thank you, Senator Corker.

I understand that a class from Jefferson High School of Alexandria, VA, is with us. We welcome you all to the Senate Foreign Relations Committee today. It is a great topic for you to be listening to as we move in the course of events here. So, welcome.

Our first panel, we have Mary McLeod, the State Department's Principal Deputy Legal Adviser, and Stephen Preston, the General Counsel of the Department of Defense.

Your full statements will be included in the record, without objection. I would ask you to summarize those statements in about 5 minutes or so, so that the members can engage you in a question-and-answer session.

And, with that, Ms. McLeod, you are recognized.

STATEMENT OF MARY E. McLEOD, PRINCIPAL DEPUTY LEGAL ADVISER, U.S. DEPARTMENT OF STATE, WASHINGTON, DC

Ms. McLEOD. Thank you very much, Chairman Menendez, Ranking Member Corker, and members of the committee, for the invitation to speak at this hearing. The administration looks forward to engaging with this committee and the Congress on this important topic.

I will begin with some introductory remarks before discussing briefly a few international law aspects of the administration's legal framework for conducting operations pursuant to the 2001 Authorization for Use of Military Force, or AUMF. I will conclude by laying out a few relevant considerations first, establishing our legal framework beyond 2014. My colleague, Stephen Preston, General Counsel of the Department of Defense, will then address the current framework under U.S. law for military counterterrorism operations.

As an initial matter, as you have noted, the President has made clear his desire to engage with Congress about the future of the AUMF. The President expressed his commitment to move America off a permanent war footing, 1 year ago, in his speech at the National Defense University, and reaffirmed that commitment in this year's State of the Union Address. And the President made clear in his NDU speech that his goal is to engage with Congress and the American people to refine and ultimately repeal the AUMF.

As we begin our dialogue on this issue, it will be critical to assess our legal authorities, not only within the context of our current military operations, but also in light of future needs, which, as of today's hearing, may not be fully apparent. At the same time, as the President has said, we must keep in mind, going forward, that not every collection of thugs that label themselves al-Qaeda will pose a threat to the United States that requires the use of military force in response.

Turning now to international legal considerations. As we consider the future of the AUMF, it will be critical to ensure that U.S. actions continue to be grounded firmly in international law. Under international law, the United States has an inherent right of self-defense to use force to respond to an armed attack or to the imminent threat of an armed attack. And when in an armed conflict, the United States may use force, in accordance with the Law of War, to prosecute that conflict. Our use of military force must comply with international laws' requirements of necessity, proportionality, distinction, and humanity. United States use of force abroad is carried out in furtherance of these international law rights and requirements, and the Law of War specifically has and will continue to provide the legal framework for U.S. military actions taken in the armed conflict against al-Qaeda, Taliban, and associated forces. Going forward, the Office of the Legal Adviser at the State Department will continue to work to ensure that we exercise our rights consistent with these and other applicable international law principles.

I also want to note that there is a firm basis in international law to support our friends and partners facing the threat of terrorism within their own borders. Even where violent extremists pose a greater threat to those countries than they do to the United States, we can draw from all elements of national power, including military force in appropriate cases, to help them counter these threats.

In Mali, for example, we have been providing military aid to French forces to push back terrorists and other extremists. As the President stated in his speech 1 year ago, we must define our effort not as a boundless global war on terror, but, rather, as a series of persistent, targeted efforts to dismantle specific networks of violent extremists that threaten America. Indeed, targeted efforts undertaken in partnership with other countries can be highly effective in countering terrorist threats without keeping the United States on a permanent wartime footing.

With these principles in mind, let me now outline a few considerations regarding a future legal framework. We are currently working to identify an appropriate United States military presence in Afghanistan after 2014. We are also working toward the closure of the detention facility at Guantanamo Bay, which the President has reaffirmed will further our national security, our international standing, and our ability to cooperate with allies in counterterrorism efforts. We also continue to work with our allies and partners to provide assistance and training to increase our capacity to take effective measures against terrorist organizations. The State Department is joined by many other U.S. agencies in implementing this comprehensive strategy, which includes a broad range of military and other foreign assistance, law enforcement cooperation, intelligence-sharing, and diplomatic engagement. All of these efforts are vital to countering threats. This is true even at times such as the present, when we are using military force as part of our response to the terrorist threat. In the long term, the success of our efforts will depend not exclusively on the use of military force, but also on sustained attention to achieving effective governance and the rule of law in countries where terrorist threats proliferate.

And, based on all these considerations, we would suggest that our efforts to identify a future legal framework be guided by the following principles.

First, any domestic authority that we rely on to use military force should reflect the President's clear direction that we must move America off a permanent wartime footing. As the President stated, this means that we will engage with Congress and the American people to refine, and ultimately repeal, the AUMF, and that the President will not sign a law designed to expand the AUMF's mandate further.

Second, any authorization to use military force, including any detention operations, must be consistent with international law.

Third, we must continue to enhance our cooperation with partner nations to take action within their own borders, including law enforcement action and other forms of engagement, where those methods provide the most effective and sustainable means of countering terrorist threats.

Finally, we must keep in mind that the President's authority to defend the United States would remain part of any framework that emerges.

Thank you very much. And I will now turn to Stephen Preston to make his statement. And, after that, we would be happy to answer any questions you may have.

[The prepared statement of Ms. McLeod follows:]

PREPARED STATEMENT OF MARY E. MCLEOD

Thank you very much Chairman Menendez, Ranking Member Corker, and members of the committee, for the invitation to speak at this hearing. The administration looks forward to engaging with this committee and the Congress on this important topic.

I will begin with some introductory remarks before discussing briefly a few international law aspects of the administration's legal framework for conducting operations pursuant to the 2001 Authorization for Use of Military Force (AUMF). I will conclude by laying out a few relevant considerations for establishing our legal framework beyond 2014. My colleague Stephen Preston, General Counsel of the Department of Defense, will then address the current framework under U.S. law for military counterterrorism operations.

As an initial matter, the President has made clear his desire to engage with Congress about the future of the AUMF. The President expressed his commitment to ''move [America] off a permanent war footing'' 1 year ago in his speech at the National Defense University (NDU), and reaffirmed this commitment in this year's State of the Union address. And the President made clear in his NDU speech that his goal is to engage with Congress and the American people to ''refine, and ultimately repeal'' the AUMF.

As we begin our dialogue on this issue, it will be critical to assess our legal authorities not only within the context of our current military operations, but also in light of future needs, which as of today's hearing may not be fully apparent. At the same time, as the President has said, we must keep in mind going forward that not every collection of thugs that label themselves al-Qaeda will pose a threat to the United States that requires the use of military force in response.

INTERNATIONAL LEGAL CONSIDERATIONS

Turning now to international legal considerations, as we consider the future of the AUMF, it will be critical to ensure that U.S. actions continue to be grounded firmly in international law. Under international law, the United States has an inherent right of self-defense to use force to respond to an armed attack, or the imminent threat of an armed attack. And, when in an armed conflict, the United States may use force, in accordance with the law of war, to prosecute that conflict. Our use of military force must comply with international law's requirements of necessity, proportionality, distinction, and humanity.

United States use of force abroad is carried out in furtherance of these international law rights and requirements, and the law of war specifically has and will continue to provide the legal framework for U.S. military actions taken in the armed conflict against al-Qaeda, Taliban, and associated forces. Going forward, the Office of the Legal Adviser at the State Department will continue to work to ensure that we exercise our rights consistent with these and other applicable international law principles.

I also want to note that there is a firm basis in international law to support our friends and partners facing the threat of terrorism within their own borders. Even where violent extremists pose a greater threat to these countries than they do to the United States, we can draw from all elements of national power—including military force, in appropriate cases—to help them counter these threats. In Mali, for example, we have been providing military aid to French forces to push back terrorists and other extremists. As the President stated in his speech 1 year ago, "we must define our effort not as a boundless global war on terror, but rather as a series of persistent, targeted efforts to dismantle specific networks of violent extremists that threaten America." Indeed, targeted efforts undertaken in partnership with other countries can be highly effective in countering terrorist threats, without keeping the United States on a permanent wartime footing.

POST-2014 LEGAL FRAMEWORK

With these principles in mind, let me now outline a few considerations regarding a future legal framework. We are currently working to identify an appropriate U.S. military presence in Afghanistan after 2014. We are also working toward the closure of the detention facility at Guantanamo Bay, which the President has reaffirmed will further our national security, our international standing, and our ability to cooperate with allies in counterterrorism efforts. We also continue to work with our allies and partners to provide assistance and training to increase their capacity to take effective measures against terrorist organizations.

The State Department is joined by many other U.S. agencies in implementing this comprehensive strategy, which includes a broad range of military and other foreign assistance, law enforcement cooperation, intelligence-sharing, and diplomatic engagement. All of these efforts are vital to countering threats. This is true even at times—such as the present—when we are using military force as part of our response to the terrorist threat. In the long term, the success of our efforts will depend not exclusively on the use of military force, but also on sustained attention to achieving effective governance and the rule of law in countries where terrorist threats proliferate.

We also bear in mind what Department of Homeland Security Secretary Jeh Johnson, then in his capacity as General Counsel of the Department of Defense, stated in his November 2012 speech at the Oxford Union. He noted that there will come a "tipping point" when our efforts to disrupt, dismantle, and defeat al-Qaeda have succeeded to such an extent that we will no longer describe ourselves as being in an "armed conflict" with al-Qaeda to which the law of war applies. At that point, we will rely primarily on law enforcement, intelligence, foreign assistance, and diplomatic means—in cooperation with the international community—to counter any remaining threat posed by al-Qaeda and its affiliates. And as we do so, we will retain the authority, under both international and domestic law, to act in national or collective self-defense against armed attacks or imminent threats thereof posed by terrorist groups.

Based on all of these considerations, we would suggest that our efforts to identify a future legal framework be guided by the following principles:

- First, any domestic authority that we rely on to use military force should reflect the President's clear direction that we must move America off a permanent wartime footing. As the President stated, this means that we will engage with Congress and the American people to "refine, and ultimately repeal" the AUMF, and that the President will not sign a law designed to expand the AUMF's mandate further.

- Second, any authorization to use military force, including any detention operations, must be consistent with international law.
- Third, we must continue to enhance our cooperation with partner nations to take action within their own borders, including law enforcement action and other forms of engagement, where those methods provide the most effective and sustainable means of countering terrorist threats.
- Fourth, the President has made clear that now is the time to close the detention facility at Guantanamo Bay, and any future legislation should lift all remaining restrictions on the Commander in Chief's authority to transfer detainees held under the law of war.
- Finally, we must keep in mind that the President's authority to defend the United States would remain part of any framework that emerges.

Thank you very much. I will now turn to Stephen Preston to make his statement. After that, we would be happy to address any questions you might have.

The CHAIRMAN. Mr. Preston.

STATEMENT OF HON. STEPHEN W. PRESTON, GENERAL COUNSEL, U.S. DEPARTMENT OF DEFENSE, WASHINGTON, DC

Mr. PRESTON. Thank you, Mr. Chairman, Ranking Member Corker, and members of the committee. Appreciate this opportunity to appear.

I would like to open with a brief discussion of the current legal framework for U.S. military operations, focusing on how the 2001 Authorization for the Use of Military Force is being applied by the Department of Defense.

Although the AUMF makes no express mention of specific nations or groups, it was clearly intended to authorize the President to use force against al-Qaeda, the organization that perpetrated the 9/11 attacks, and the Taliban, which harbored al-Qaeda. In addition, based on the well-established concept of cobelligerency in the laws of war, the AUMF has been interpreted to authorize the use of force against associated forces of al-Qaeda and the Taliban.

As the administration has stated publicly on numerous occasions, to be an associated force, a group must be both an organized, armed group that has entered the fight alongside al-Qaeda or the Taliban and a cobelligerent with al-Qaeda or the Taliban in hostilities against the United States or its coalition partners.

The Department of Defense relies on the AUMF in three contexts: ongoing United States military operations in Afghanistan, our ongoing military operations against al-Qaeda and associated forces outside the United States in the theater of Afghanistan, and detention operations in Afghanistan and at the Guantanamo Bay, Cuba, facility.

In Afghanistan, the U.S. military currently conducts operations pursuant to the AUMF against al-Qaeda, the Taliban, and other terrorist or insurgent groups that are engaged alongside al-Qaeda and the Taliban in hostilities against the United States and its coalition partners. In addition, the ISAF and U.S. rules of engagement permit the targeting of hostile personnel in Afghanistan, based on the threat they pose to United States, coalition, and Afghan forces or to civilians.

Outside the United States in areas of active hostilities, the U.S. military currently takes direct action under the AUMF—that is, capture and lethal operations—in the following circumstances.

First, in Yemen, the United States military has conducted direct action targeting members of al-Qaeda in the Arabian Peninsula. AQAP is an organized, armed group that is part of al-Qaeda, or at least an associated force of al-Qaeda, for purposes of the AUMF.

Second, the United States military has also conducted capture or lethal operations under the AUMF outside Afghanistan against individuals who are part of al-Qaeda and targeted as such. For example, in Somalia, the United States military has conducted direct action against a limited number of targets who have been determined to be part of al-Qaeda. And in Libya, in October 2013, in reliance on the AUMF, United States Forces captured longtime al-Qaeda member Abu Anas al-Libi.

Now, the fact that an al-Qaeda-affiliated group has not to date been identified as an associated force for purposes of the AUMF does not mean that the United States has made a final determination that the group is not an associated force. We are prepared to review this question whenever a situation arises in which it may be necessary to take direct action against a terrorist group in order to protect our country.

Lastly, in our ongoing armed conflict against al-Qaeda, the Taliban, and associated forces, the United States military relies on the authority of the AUMF to hold enemy belligerents in military detention in Afghanistan and at the detention facility at Guantanamo Bay.

The AUMF is not the only authority the President has to use force to keep us safe. For example, the President has authority, under the United States Constitution, to use military force as needed to defend the Nation against armed attacks or imminent threats of armed attack. This inherent right of self-defense is also recognized in international law.

Looking forward, the central question is, What future legal framework will provide the authorities necessary in order for our government to meet the terrorist threat to our country, but will not greatly exceed what is needed to meet the threat? As was made clear in the President's NDU speech last year, the answer is not legislation granting the Executive unbound powers more suited for traditional armed conflicts between nation-states. Rather, the objective is a framework that will support a series of persistent, targeted efforts to dismantle specific networks of violent extremists that threaten America. The challenge is to ensure that the authorities for U.S. military operations are both adequate and appropriately tailored to the threat.

And, with that, I look forward to answering your questions.

[The prepared statement of Mr. Preston follows:]

PREPARED STATEMENT OF STEPHEN W. PRESTON

Thank you, Chairman Menendez, Ranking Member Corker, and members of the committee, for this opportunity to testify about the framework under U.S. law for ongoing military counterterrorism and detention operations. Following up on the remarks of my colleague from the Department of State, I will discuss (i) the executive branch's interpretation of the 2001 Authorization for the Use of Military Force (AUMF); (ii) how the AUMF is being applied by the Department of Defense in the armed conflict against al-Qaeda, the Taliban, and associated forces; and (iii) other domestic legal authority available to defend our country against terrorist threats.

10

The AUMF, enacted 1 week after the attacks of September 11, 2001, authorizes the President to use "all necessary and appropriate force against those nations, organizations, or persons he determines planned, authorized, committed, or aided the terrorist attacks that occurred on September 11, 2001, or harbored such organizations or persons, in order to prevent any future acts of international terrorism against the United States by such nations, organizations, or persons." The executive branch interprets the AUMF to authorize the use of force against al-Qaeda, the Taliban, and associated forces. This interpretation has been embraced by the courts in the context of habeas corpus litigation involving detainees at the Guantanamo Bay detention facility, and by the Congress when it codified the interpretation, for the purposes of detention, almost word for word in Section 1021 of the National Defense Authorization Act for Fiscal Year 2012.

Although the AUMF makes no express mention of specific nations or groups, it was clearly intended to authorize the use of force against al-Qaeda, the "organization" that "planned, authorized, committed, and aided the terrorist attacks that occurred on September 11, 2001," as well as the Taliban, which "harbored" al-Qaeda. The concept of an "associated force" is based on the well-established concept of cobelligerency in the laws of war.

As the administration has stated publicly on numerous occasions, to be an "associated force," a group must be both (1) an organized, armed group that has entered the fight alongside al-Qaeda or the Taliban and (2) a cobelligerent with al-Qaeda or the Taliban in hostilities against the United States or its coalition partners. Before a group may be targeted for direct action under the AUMF, it is evaluated against this standard based on its current and historical activities. The determination that a particular group is an "associated force" is made at the most senior levels of the U.S. Government, following reviews by senior government lawyers and informed by departments and agencies with relevant expertise and institutional roles, including all-source intelligence from the U.S. intelligence community. It is not the case in law or in practice that the concept of an "associated force" is open-ended or otherwise provides the administration with unlimited flexibility to define the scope of the AUMF. A group that simply embraces al-Qaeda's ideology is not an "associated force," nor is every group or individual that commits terrorist acts.

II. CURRENT APPLICATION OF THE AUMF

The Department of Defense relies on the AUMF in three contexts: for ongoing U.S. military operations in Afghanistan; for our ongoing military operations against al-Qaeda and associated forces outside of the United States and the theater of Afghanistan; and for associated detention operations in Afghanistan and at the detention facility at Guantanamo Bay, Cuba.

Operations in Afghanistan

In Afghanistan, the U.S. military currently conducts operations pursuant to the AUMF against al-Qaeda, the Taliban, and other terrorist and insurgent groups that are engaged alongside al-Qaeda and the Taliban in hostilities against the United States or its coalition partners. In addition, the International Security Assistance Force and U.S. rules of engagement permit targeting of hostile personnel in Afghanistan based on the threat they pose to U.S., coalition, and Afghan forces or to civilians.

Beyond 2014, assuming we are able to conclude the Bilateral Security Agreement (BSA) with the Afghan Government on an acceptable timeline, the United States would seek to retain a small military presence in Afghanistan to conduct two narrow missions. First, to provide limited noncombat support to train, advise, and assist the Afghan National Security Forces under a North Atlantic Treaty Organization regional framework. And, second, to provide a U.S. national capability to disrupt terrorist activity in that region. The continued presence of U.S. forces in Afghanistan would be conditioned not only on the conclusion of the BSA, but also on the timely and smooth political transition to a post-Karzai administration sometime this year.

Counterterrorism Operations Outside the United States and Areas of Active Hostilities

For operations outside Afghanistan, as the President announced in his speech at National Defense University on May 23, 2013, he has issued Presidential Policy Guidance to formalize and strengthen the administration's rigorous standards and procedures for reviewing and approving operations to capture or employ lethal force against terrorist targets outside the United States and outside areas of active hostilities. Pursuant to this Guidance, when the U.S. military takes lethal counterterrorism action beyond the Afghan theater, it does so only against targets that both are lawful military targets under domestic and international law and pose a continuing, imminent threat to U.S. persons. Thus, under the President's policy, no one is targeted with lethal military force outside Afghanistan based solely on membership in al-Qaeda or an associated force. In addition, this Guidance requires near certainty that noncombatants will not be killed or injured before lethal action may be taken.

The U.S. military currently takes direct action (capture or lethal operations) under the AUMF outside the United States and areas of active hostilities in the following circumstances:

- First, in Yemen, the U.S. military has conducted direct action targeting members of Al Qaeda in the Arabian Peninsula (AQAP), which is an organized, armed group that is part of, or at least an associated force of, al-Qaeda. The determination that the AUMF authorizes the use of force against AQAP is based on information about both AQAP's current and historical connections to al-Qaeda and the fact that AQAP has repeatedly launched attacks against the United States, including the December 2009 "underwear bomber" attack and the 2010 "printer cartridge" attack. In addition, AQAP continues to plan and attempt attacks against U.S. persons, both inside and outside Yemen.
- Second, the U.S. military has also conducted capture or lethal operations under the AUMF outside of Afghanistan against individuals who are part of al-Qaeda and targeted as such. For example, in Somalia, the U.S. military has conducted direct action against a limited number of targets who, based on information about their current and historical activities, have been determined to be part of al-Qaeda. (Some of these individuals are also part of al-Shabaab, a group that is openly affiliated with al-Qaeda.) In Libya, in October 2013, in reliance on the AUMF, U.S. forces captured longtime al-Qaeda member Abu Anas al Libi.

The fact that an al-Qaeda-affiliated group has not been identified as an "associated force" for purposes of the AUMF does not mean that the United States has made a final determination that the group is not an "associated force." We are prepared to review this question whenever a situation arises in which it may be necessary to take direct action against a terrorist group.

Detention Operations

Lastly, in our ongoing armed conflict against al-Qaeda, the Taliban, and associated forces, the U.S. military relies on the authority of the AUMF to hold enemy belligerents in military detention in Afghanistan and at the detention facility at Guantanamo Bay, Cuba.

III. OTHER DOMESTIC LEGAL AUTHORITY

For more than 12 years, the AUMF has provided authority to defend against certain known terrorist threats to our country—those posed by al-Qaeda, the Taliban, and associated forces—notably, those groups and associated forces in Afghanistan, AQAP in Yemen, and individuals who are part of al-Qaeda elsewhere such as Somalia and Libya. However, the AUMF is not the only authority the President has to use force in order to keep us safe. For example, the President has authority, under the U.S. Constitution, to use military force as needed to defend the nation against armed attacks and imminent threats of armed attack. (This inherent right of national self-defense is also recognized in international law.) Thus, although we are strongest when Congress and the executive branch are acting together, the President has the authority to respond to emerging threats, should it become necessary to do so.

A central question looking forward is what future legal framework will provide the authorities necessary in order for our government to meet the terrorist threat to our country, but will not greatly exceed what is needed to meet that threat. As was made clear in the President's NDU speech last year, the answer is not legislation granting the Executive "unbound powers more suited for traditional armed conflicts between nations." Rather, the objective is a framework that will support "a series of persistent, targeted efforts to dismantle specific networks of violent extremists that threaten America." The challenge is to ensure that the authorities for U.S. military counterterrorism and detention operations are both adequate and appropriately tailored to the threat.

It is also essential that we strive for clarity in the legal authority for, and associated restrictions on, the use of military force. Such clarity is necessary to ensure the lawfulness of our government's actions, first and foremost, and in efforts to explain the legal framework on which we would rely to the American public and to the United States partners abroad.

The CHAIRMAN. Well, thank you both. I know you stuck to your script, so let me try to get you off your script and go back to my original questions.

Is the 9/11 AUMF broken in some way? Is it obsolete? Is it inadequate to the threats we and our friends and allies face today and in the foreseeable future?

I offer that up for either one of you to answer, or both of you to answer.

Mr. PRESTON. Let me begin, Mr. Chairman, and say that I agree with the views expressed on behalf of DOD, a little more than a year ago in a hearing before the Senate Armed Services Committee, that the AUMF is adequate in order to prosecute and continue to prosecute the current armed conflict against al-Qaeda, the Taliban, and associated forces.

To the extent that the United States is threatened by a terrorist group to which the AUMF has not been determined to apply, the President, as we have said, has authority, under the U.S. Constitution, to defend the Nation against armed attacks and imminent threats of such attacks, and therefore, has the authority to use military force against groups in order to protect the country from that threat.

The CHAIRMAN. Is it obsolete in any way?

Mr. PRESTON. Well, I think, as the President has observed, we have reached a time, now 12 years into the conflict, where it is appropriate to review the AUMF with an eye toward its refinement and, ultimately, its repeal. In my view, I would say what we are looking for, and looking to develop, is a legal framework for the future that will enable us to continue fighting the terrorists that threaten our country and, at the same time, to take the country off a permanent wartime footing.

The CHAIRMAN. All right, let me ask you a series of questions to further define this. One is specifically that I hope can have a relatively easy answer, which is on the Iraq AUMF. The United States ended its combat operations in Iraq in 2010, and, in fact, withdrew all of its military forces that same year. Since then, Congress has, on a number of occasions, examined the possibility of repealing the 2002 AUMF authorizing our Iraq operations, but the administration has repeatedly opposed those efforts.

Starting with you, Ms. McLeod, can you explain to the committee, one, whether the administration continues to oppose repeal of the Iraq AUMF? And, if so, why? And I would like to hear your answer to this, Mr. Preston, as well.

Ms. MCLEOD. Certainly, Chairman Menendez. And, once again, thank you for inviting me to testify here today.

As you said, the United States has ended combat operations in Iraq, and we have withdrawn our military forces. And I can confirm that we are not relying on the 2002 Iraq AUMF for any military operations, nor do we intend to do so. And I am here to tell you today that the administration now supports repeal of the 2002 IraqAUMF.

Mr. PRESTON. Mr. Chairman, I agree. That is certainly my understanding, as well.

The CHAIRMAN. All right. That brings to full circle my view, which we should not have been in Iraq in the first place. That is why I voted against it. And I would be happy to repeal it now.

Expressions of approval or disapproval of any of the statements that take place in this hearing are inappropriate, and I would urge the audience to act accordingly.

My second question is one I would like for both of you to answer. If the AUMF were to expire, would the President be able to conduct counterterror operations, such as drone strikes in Yemen or other operations against the perpetrators of the Benghazi attack, using existing legal authorities? Or would a new or amended AUMF be required to conduct such operations?

Ms. MCLEOD. Thank you, Mr. Chairman. Let me begin.

The AUMF currently, as we have said, authorizes the use of force against al-Qaeda, Taliban, and associated forces. And in Yemen, the U.S. military has conducted direct action targeting members of Al Qaeda in the Arabian Peninsula, known as AQAP, which has been determined to be, at least, either part of or at least associated with al-Qaeda. And, as you mentioned, Senator, Article 2 of the Constitution provides the President with the authority to target with military force those who pose an imminent threat of armed attack against the United States. And, as both a domestic law matter and an international law matter, this authority to act in self-defense does not depend on the existence of an AUMF.

With respect to the AUMF, though, in particular, we are still in an armed conflict, as of today, with al-Qaeda, Taliban, and associated forces. And the AUMF continues to provide a source of authority to use military force against those groups, when necessary, including associated detention operations.

And I would also note that the—as I said in my statement—that the President has and uses a range of other authorities to counter terrorist threats, and these law enforcement, intelligence, foreign assistance authorities——

The CHAIRMAN. So, your answer——

Ms. MCLEOD [continuing]. And so forth.

The CHAIRMAN. Just to synthesize it for me, because I know, when I deal with lawyers, I have to get to—is—your answer, therefore, is, you do not need a new—from your view, a new or amended AUMF to conduct such operations.

Ms. MCLEOD. Not for the President to take action against imminent threats to the United States.

The CHAIRMAN. Is that your view, Mr. Preston?

Mr. PRESTON. I agree.

The CHAIRMAN. Now, the question is, Is acting against the perpetrators of Benghazi's attack an imminent threat?

[Pause.]

The CHAIRMAN. I would be happy for either one of you to answer.

Ms. MCLEOD. We will answer. I will——

The CHAIRMAN. I know, because I am not going to go to the next Senator until you do, so——

[Laughter.]

Ms. MCLEOD. Okay. No, I promise, I am going to answer right now.

Senator, the United States remains committed to using every lawful tool available to bring the perpetrators of the Benghazi attacks to justice. And we think we have adequate tools to meet that objective.

The CHAIRMAN. You think you have adequate tools meet that objective.

Ms. MCLEOD. Yes.

The CHAIRMAN. And can you give me a sense of what those tools are?

Ms. MCLEOD. Well, the administration favors bringing those responsible for the attacks to justice through prosecution in an Article 3 court. And the Justice Department is conducting an investigation to try and achieve that end.

The CHAIRMAN. Yes. And if that investigation leads to the identification of perpetrators, how would you act against the perpetrators? Under what authority?

Mr. PRESTON. Sir, perhaps I could chime and say——

The CHAIRMAN. Yes.

Mr. PRESTON [continuing]. I think we have a range of authorities. And our government is committed to making full use of all lawfully available instruments of national power to bring these people to justice and to ensure that they do not present a threat to this country.

To the extent that they present an imminent threat of violent attack to this country, the President has, under the Constitution, authority to use force in order to protect this country. Beyond that, to the extent we are presented with a concrete situation, we are in a position to evaluate and reevaluate whether they would qualify under the AUMF. And, in addition, quite apart from the use of military force and those authorities, there is law enforcement authority to apprehend and bring to justice, try, and prosecute these criminals.

The CHAIRMAN. Let me ask you two final questions before I turn to Senator Corker.

What authorities does the 9/11 AUMF give the President, in terms of authorities to use force, that he does not already possess in other authorities, including Article 2 of the Constitution?

Ms. MCLEOD. Senator, as we have said, the President does have authority, under Article 2, to protect the Nation against imminent threat of armed attack. However, as the President has said, and I agree with, it is always better and more powerful to have the executive branch and Congress working together on issues involving——

The CHAIRMAN. Yes, that is not my question. My question is very simple.

In order to determine what we do, moving forward—I do not mean to interrupt you, but—I have got to get a sense, at least from an administration perspective, of what you feel the AUMF gave you that you did not have otherwise, constitutionally or through some other statutory provisions. Because if you tell me that you have all the authorities in the world to go ahead and do everything that the 9/11 AUMF provided, then that AUMF was not necessary. So, give me a sense of what you got through the AUMF that you do not have under existing constitutional or statutory law.

Mr. PRESTON. Senator, if I might answer that, I think it would be fair to say that, with or without an AUMF, to the extent that it grants authority for the use of military force against al-Qaeda and the Taliban and associated forces in which we are in armed conflict, and to the extent that those groups continue to pose an imminent threat of violent attack to this country, the President does have constitutional authority to act. It is not——

The CHAIRMAN. So, you are telling us, that AUMF was not necessary.

Mr. PRESTON. No, sir.

The CHAIRMAN. Other than an expression of congressional support for that engagement.

Mr. PRESTON. Not an unimportant point, Mr. Chairman, but I think the point is that these two sources of authority are not, and I do not think were ever intended to be, mutually exclusive. And, in fact, as your question suggests, they are very largely overlapping when it comes to groups that present a terrorist threat of attack to this country.

I am not going to tell you there are no differences between the two. The concept between an Authorization for the Use of Military Force, which names enemy groups and, similar to Law of War concepts, enables the use of force against groups, including to degrade those forces, without specific reference to imminent threat, is not the same concept or approach as the President's constitutional authority to defend the country against imminent threat, and that parallel international law concept of national self-defense in which it is rooted in the presence of imminent threat.

But, I think, in terms of the authority to protect this country against these groups, at least some of which present a threat of imminent attack against the United States, both the statute and the Constitution provide authority for the President to use military force to protect us.

The CHAIRMAN. Senator Corker.

Senator CORKER. Mr. Chairman, I have to say, I know several of us were involved in a very bizarre discussion last night. This continues a very bizarre discussion.

I do want to say, for those who are reading the transcripts, Ms. McLeod, it is unbelievable to me that, to answer our questions, you have to find the place, a pre-prepared statement to make, and cannot answer these questions directly yourself, which is troubling to me. But, let me just—I think what you have said, if I can synthesize the legalese that you have used, is that the President needs no AUMF to carry out the the counterterrorism activities we are carrying out around the world. If I heard you correctly, I think that is what you said. Is that correct?

Ms. McLEOD. Senator, I think what I said was, he has authority to use military force if it is necessary.

Senator CORKER. I think what I heard you say is, he has the authority to carry out the activities he is carrying without really having an AUMF. And Mr. President—Mr. Preston, with a degree of legalese, has, I think, said something similar. I would just like to know, yes or no: If the 2001 AUMF was undone, can the President carry out the activities that he is carrying out right now?

Ms. McLEOD. Yes, I believe he could, Senator Corker. But——

Senator CORKER. So, we have really——

Ms. MCLEOD [continuing]. I do think——

Senator CORKER [continuing]. As a Congress, do not need to be involved in this subject at all.

Ms. MCLEOD. What I was going to say, in addition, is that I think, when we are talking about sustained military engagements, it is definitely appropriate to get Authorizations for Use of Military Force.

Senator CORKER. Are we in sustained——

Ms. MCLEOD. And that has been the practice——

Senator CORKER [continuing]. Military operations now against terrorists?

Ms. MCLEOD [continuing]. Certainly against——

Senator CORKER. I know the President, a year ago, said we were not. We were doing targeted—I forgot the phraseology that he used. And maybe it was to circumvent this, I do not know. But, are we, or are we not, in a continuous effort against al-Qaeda and affiliated groups? Yes or no?

[Pause.]

Senator CORKER. I would like for the record—she has to——

Mr. PRESTON. Yes, we are.

Senator CORKER [continuing]. Look at the other person to get the answer. I find this very disconcerting today. Do you want to— I guess you want to answer it for her?

Mr. PRESTON. I am sorry, I did not understand your question was directed solely at her.

Senator CORKER. Well, let me, Ms. McLeod, since you are at State Department and that is who we have jurisdiction over—and I noticed a staffer has given you the answer, there. If you would read it for us, it would be great.

Ms. MCLEOD. Could you repeat your question, Senator Corker?

Senator CORKER. Does the President have the ability, without an AUMF, to carry out the activities that he is carrying out today against terrorists, affiliates of al-Qaeda? And are we, or are we not, engaged in continuous activity against them?

Ms. MCLEOD. We continue to be in an armed conflict with al-Qaeda——

Senator CORKER. So, we are in continuous activity. So, do we need an AUMF, or not?

[Pause.]

Ms. MCLEOD. I think, as we have said, it is important to have——

Senator CORKER. Important for what reason, politically or legally?

Ms. MCLEOD. In part, politically, but also because, when the Congress has a role to play——

Senator CORKER. Well, tell me what that role is. Because if I understand what you said before, the President can carry out the activities he is carrying out without an AUMF. So, it sounds to me like we are pretty irrelevant to the process from the administration's standpoint.

Ms. MCLEOD. That is not true, Senator Corker.

Senator CORKER. Well, tell me——

Ms. MCLEOD. We have——

Senator CORKER [continuing]. How we are relevant.

Ms. McLEOD [continuing]. Consulted closely with the Congress on our counterterrorism activities.

Senator CORKER. Okay.

Well, let me ask—let me change topics. I am really—this is not the line of questioning I expected, but I also expected a different type of testimony today on one of the most important issues that our Nation deals with.

But, Mr. President, do you think—Mr. Preston, excuse me—do you believe that the 9/11 AUMF authorizes you to take action against all terrorist groups that present an ongoing serious threat to the United States? Are there any terrorist groups that you think the AUMF does not—it sounds like you all do not think we need an AUMF at all, so it is kind of becoming an irrelevant question. But, are there terrorist groups, per the AUMF that you do not think it is relevant, that you do not have the ability to go against?

Mr. PRESTON. Senator, I would not say the AUMF is irrelevant or that Congress's role is irrelevant. The point we were trying— that I was trying to make is that there is very robust authority, both in the AUMF and in the Article 2, in terms of the President's powers——

Senator CORKER. Are there other groups that we cannot go against today, yes or no?

Mr. PRESTON. Yes, sir. The—I mean, let me finish the point, which is to say, the President has invited us to focus and engage in dialogue with Congress about the continued necessity and utility of the AUMF or a follow-on legal regime.

To answer your question more directly, the AUMF applies to al-Qaeda, Taliban, groups and individuals that are part of al-Qaeda and the Taliban, and associated——

Senator CORKER. That was not the question. And you are really frustrating me.

Mr. PRESTON. There are——

Senator CORKER. And I have a generally good nature, but I am really getting upset. Okay?

Are there groups today that the administration cannot go against because the AUMF does not allow you to do that? Terrorist groups.

Mr. PRESTON. Senator Corker, I am not aware of any foreign terrorist group that presents a threat of violent attack on this country that the President lacks authority to use military force to defend against, as necessary, simply because they have not been determined to be an associated force within the AUMF.

In other words, if a group that is not, or may not be, covered by the AUMF presents a threat of violent attack to this country, the President does have authority to take action, including military action, to protect the country from that threat.

Senator CORKER. So, there are groups that did not exist at the time but are affiliated with the al-Qaeda that today are covered by the 9/11 AUMF, even though they did not exist at the time.

Mr. PRESTON. That is correct, sir. The way I look at it is, the AUMF, not by name, but essentially identified the Taliban and al-Qaeda as our enemies, and that other groups, most notably AQAP, which has emerged since that time, have made themselves our enemy by joining with al-Qaeda and engaging in hostilities against our country.

Senator CORKER. Yes. So, the group that I discussed in my opening comments, ISIS, which is split from al-Qaeda, that is not affiliated with al-Qaeda—and actually, I heard administration officials had expressed concerns about their ability to deal with them in Syria and as they migrate back across into Iraq. Are you saying that, even though they are not a part of al-Qaeda, you have the authority to go against them?

Mr. PRESTON. Senator, what we would do if we were presented with a need and an opportunity of contemplating the use of military force would be to examine what our authorities were. That would consist, first of all, of determining whether or not they would fall within the AUMF as an associated force, using the definition that we have provided, or, if not, if they present a threat of imminent attack on this country, we could rely on the President's inherent constitutional authority.

Senator CORKER. So, you would not rely on the AUMF. He just has authority to do whatever.

Mr. PRESTON. We could rely on the AUMF to the extent that this group, or any other group, is covered by the AUMF.

Senator CORKER. But—I thought you just—yes.

Mr. Chairman, I find this bizarre, and I hope that our next group of witnesses is a little more clear.

I do want to say that both of you indicated the President has asked you to engage with Congress on this. To my knowledge— I am the ranking member of this committee, and, along with other members on this committee, have expressed interest in the AUMF for some time. I have had no reachout from the administration. My guess is, the chairman has not. I would love to know if Tim or anybody else has. I know everybody's expressed concern.

So, that is another line of hollow comments from this administration. You have reached out in no way to talk to us about refining this. I understand you guys want to refine and replace some— or repeal—refine and repeal. And I do hope, at some point, you will define what that is. But, this is a hearing that is not particularly gratifying, and I do look forward to talking to you more in the future.

Mr. PRESTON. Sir, we look forward to engaging with you and the committee and the other committees, as well. I will say, since the President's speech, the administration has devoted a great deal of energy to focusing on the drawdown in Afghanistan and what the mission and presence will be there, to redouble the effort to clear detainees from GTMO toward the closure of that facility, implementation of policy guidance concerning counterterrorism operations outside of Afghanistan. We have tried to be in continuous dialogue with congressional committees on that, including on the BSA and such. And those are the precursors to focusing on possible repeal and, in the meantime, refinement of the AUF.

And we have made progress, particularly I can speak for we agency lawyers, in focusing on what sort of legal regime—what sort of future legal framework might govern. And we very much look forward to engaging with the committee and other committees on that when the administration is prepared to engage in that discussion in earnest.

But, a good deal of this is premised on a finalization of what the circumstances, the mission and presence, in Afghanistan will be. And that still remains to be finalized.

Senator CORKER. Mr. President—Preston—I do not know why I keep calling you "Mr. President."

Mr. PRESTON. I will try not to get used to it.

Senator CORKER. Yes. [Laughter.]

That last statement, about waiting to see what we are going to do in Afghanistan after this Presidential election, is one of the most bogus, lacking-of-substance comments I have ever heard before this committee. It has nothing—nothing to do with this AUMF. Nothing.

And I have to tell you, Mr. Chairman—I know we were involved in a discussion last night—I think the administration is totally unprepared to discuss this issue, totally unprepared to decide how many troops we are going to have in Afghanistan, continue to hide behind this Presidential race that is taking place in Afghanistan. We all know what the outcome is going to be.

And I just want to say that you discredit our country with statements like you just made, that we are waiting to see what we are going to do in Afghanistan to determine whether—or what an AUMF needs to look like. So, I am very disappointed in your testimony. I am disappointed in the White House's inability to deal with substance, but to continue to deal with the optics of the way things are going to look. And I do look forward to that engagement, whenever it occurs. It has not occurred in a long, long time.

The CHAIRMAN. Before I turn to Senator Kaine, I think Mr. Preston's comment is not necessarily—the way you took it is not necessarily the way I took it, in terms of looking at an overall AUMF. I actually have a line of questioning, but I wanted to turn to other members before, but I will want to come back to, specifically, on Afghanistan that might be, I think, what was meant.

I do want to just ask one thing, the prerogative of the Chair, before I turn to Senator Kaine so I do not lose the train of thought.

Basically, to now, what I hear is that there is no reason why the administration would oppose the repeal of the 9/11 AUMF totally, because you basically say the President has all the authorities, notwithstanding the AUMF.

Mr. PRESTON. Mr. Chairman, I think that is precisely the task that the President's put before us in his May NDU speech, which is to examine that question, whether and what would be appropriate in the way of refinement and ultimate repeal of the statute. We are not here today calling for the immediate repeal of the statute.

The CHAIRMAN. No, I know you are not calling——

Mr. PRESTON. We are here——

The CHAIRMAN [continuing]. For it, but your answers, so far, to both myself and the ranking member, would indicate that there is no—there is a view that, really, you have all the authorities, constitutionally and otherwise, outside of the AUMF.

Mr. PRESTON. I think what I am trying to address is, in terms of fundamentals and the fundamental ability to protect our country against imminent threat of attack. That is not to say that there are not pros and cons, advantages and disadvantages to having a statutory authorization versus relying on the President's authority. That is precisely what we are working through now, with the President's initiation. We are looking forward to engaging with the committee.

The CHAIRMAN. I appreciate that both of you want to preserve, to the maximum degree possible, all Presidential authorities. I get that. I understand that. But, we are trying, in a good-faith effort here, to actually be helpful, not harmful.

Senator Kaine has been very involved in this issue, and I look forward to his questions.

Senator KAINE. Thank you, Mr. Chairman.

And, to the witnesses, these are hard questions, but they are not "gotcha" questions, because we are trying to figure out what to do with a law that Congress passed. And I have a number of concerns about the AUMF. Congress put in it no temporal or geographic limitation. Congress did not put such limitations in the AUMF. Administration witnesses testified last year before the Armed Services Committee, opined pretty blithely that the war, so declared, would likely last another 25 or 30 years. I do not think that is what Congress intended.

I have concerns about the breadth of the definition that both administrations, the Bush and Obama administrations, have used about the associated entities to al-Qaeda that could be targeted.

I have concern about allowance of military action against those who intend harm against coalition partners, which is a huge group of partners. That was not part of the AUMF language.

And I have some concern that Congress rejected a notion of preemptive war in drafting the original AUMF, but the interpretation, especially of the "coalition partners" and "associated entities" phrases, have essentially allowed preemptive action in contravention to what Congress originally intended.

But, to my colleagues, this is something that I think only we can solve, because, as we have heard from administration witnesses in the Armed Services hearing last year, an Executive is comfortable with a carte blanche. Why would they not be comfortable with a carte blanche? And they are not going to move, I do not think, as expeditiously to rein in a carte blanche as we probably need to. So, if there is going to be action taken here, it is up to Congress to take it. And of course we want thoughts and guidance and opinions from the administration so that we take the right action, not the wrong action.

If a bill was introduced today—you have indicated that the administration supports the repeal of the Iraq AUMF—if a bill was introduced today to repeal the 9/14/01 AUMF, would the administration's position be: support, oppose, or "I do not know"?

Ms. McLEOD. As of today, Senator, I think the answer is, we do not know.

Senator KAINE. Is that fair, Mr. Preston?

Mr. PRESTON. What I would say, Senator Kaine, is that the prospect of repealing the AUMF is precisely what the President has functionally asked us to do, and that the administration wants to engage with Congress to decide.

Senator KAINE. So, I—and I follow that, but the——

Ms. MCLEOD. And——

Senator KAINE. Please, Ms. McLeod.

Ms. MCLEOD [continuing]. If I could just say. And I think we are not here to say that it should be repealed today, although it is clear that that is the President's ultimate goal.

Senator KAINE. Well, so I asked this question because the President did suggest that we should engage around these questions, in a speech that he gave in May have 2013. That is 1 year ago. So, as of today, 1 year later, if a bill was introduced to repeal the AUMF, the position would not be ''support,'' and the position would not be ''opposed''; in your testimony, the position would be ''I do not know what the administration's view would be about such a proposal.'' Is that—Ms. McLeod, that was your testimony.

Mr. Preston.

Mr. PRESTON. We did not come here this morning equipped to answer that question.

Senator KAINE. Okay. Let me ask this. What is the United States doing right now of importance that it could not do without the AUMF?

[Pause.]

Senator KAINE. So, let me give you some—well, please, answer, and then I have some example questions.

Mr. PRESTON. Well, I think as we discussed earlier, in terms of—the AUMF provides broad authority to use force against al-Qaeda, the Taliban——

Senator KAINE. Can I—that covers ground already covered. What is the United States doing right now that it could not do——

Mr. PRESTON [continuing]. I think——

Senator KAINE [continuing]. If there was no AUMF?

Mr. PRESTON [continuing]. In terms of the authority to use military force in order to address an imminent threat of armed attack against this country, that the President's constitutional authority would enable him to——

Senator KAINE. Right. So, that is what he can do. But, what could we not do if there was no AUMF?

Let me be more specific. Is there ample authority, without the AUMF, for follow-on U.S. military force in Afghanistan? If the AUMF did not exist, is there ample legal authority for follow-on U.S. military force presence in Afghanistan?

Mr. PRESTON. I think, sir, that that would have to be addressed with Congress. Right now, we have that authorization. Without that authorization, depending on the nature and scope of the U.S. mission post-2014, we may well need to engage with Congress, in terms—under the war powers process or otherwise.

Senator KAINE. So, the absence of an AUMF could affect the legality of United States presence in Afghanistan.

Let me ask you a second one. Would the absence of the AUMF affect the carrying out of CT operations by the Department of Defense? I know there are separate statutes dealing with CT operations by other agencies, but would the absence of an AUMF affect the carrying out of CT operations by the Department of Defense?

Mr. PRESTON. Not in terms of our ability to address imminent threat of armed attack.

Senator KAINE. So, there would not be a worry about the absence of an AUMF affecting DOD's CT operations.

Mr. PRESTON. Not for that purpose. Now, in terms of the—the fact is that our authority on which we have relied up until now has been the AUMF. So, we would have to reexamine the impact of its repeal on our ongoing operations.

Senator KAINE. So, there would be some potential effect on ongoing operations, in the absence of an AUMF, that you would——

Mr. PRESTON. There are certain——

Senator KAINE [continuing]. Want to engage with Congress——

Mr. PRESTON. And certainly—and that is, I think, what—I know for a fact—is what we are focusing on now within the administration, and looking forward to engaging with you, the committee, and other committees, in exploring.

Senator KAINE. Just so you will know, when you say, "looking forward to engaging," what we hear over here is—this is what engaging is. You know, we are—and so, when we come to a hearing and we are talking and we are told that we are—we can look forward to having somebody engage with us, it is like, "That is why we are here. That is why we are doing the hearing. We are engaging."

Let me ask a third one. Would the absence of an AU—and so, we do not like it to be deferred to a day that we may never get to. We are trying to do this right now. Would the absence of an AUMF raise legal questions about the continued detention of detainees at Guantanamo?

Mr. PRESTON. Do you want to take that?

Ms. McLEOD. We are holding the detainees, pursuant to the Law of War. So, as long as we are in an armed conflict with al-Qaeda, I think we would have authority to continue to hold them.

Senator KAINE. Okay, so if——

Mr. PRESTON. To answer——

Senator KAINE. Mr. Preston.

Mr. PRESTON [continuing]. Further answer, the AUMF does provide domestic authority for those purposes. So, I think, in the absence of an AUMF—and this is one of the issues that we are looking at—we would have to focus on what its impact is on our ability to continue to hold detainees.

Senator KAINE. So, if I could just summarize, what I have heard is, the administration does not have a current position about whether it would support an AUMF repeal. The issues of at least concern for examination, say, the administration believes it has the ability to counter imminent threats against the United States under constitutional powers or international laws of war. But, the absence of an AUMF would require some reexamination of DOD powers for certain CT operations, the continued detention of detainees at Guantanamo or domestically, the follow-on status of U.S. forces in Afghanistan. Those would be three areas where the absence of an AUMF would cause at least good lawyers to say, "We are not yet sure whether we want to repeal the AUMF."

Mr. PRESTON. Senator Kaine, those were all issues that are proper considerations and part of the mix as we focus on what the legal framework should be in the future, after Iraq and Afghanistan.

Senator KAINE. See, and this is helpful—and I will conclude, Mr. Chair—because if there is an effort to refine, we have to refine around what are the concerns. Carte blanche is a bad thing. Time to get done with the carte blanche grant of authority to the Executive. But, we do—we would want to come up—have a meaningful discussion about the particular areas—and we have just identified three—where there is at least a need to examine what might happen if the status quo were to change and there would be no AUMF.

Thank you, Mr. Chairman.

The CHAIRMAN. Thank you.

Senator Rubio.

Senator RUBIO. Thank you, Mr. Chairman.

Mr. Preston, as I think you would—others have also ceded to in their statements and—again, al-Qaeda has changed—the nature of al-Qaeda has dramatically changed over the last number of years. It is now spread to a number of different countries. Just since 2012, when we heard al-Qaeda was on the run, we have actually seen them establish safe havens in a number of places, including Syria. We are hearing reports, of course, of Iraq. Libya has become increasingly unstable. So, this is an evolving and, in many ways, more dangerous threat than it used to be.

So, let me ask you. Under the administration's interpretation of the 2001 AUMF, which of these affiliates are we currently authorized or able to use all necessary and appropriate force against? Which of the al-Qaeda affiliates are we authorized to use force against under the existing AUMF?

Mr. PRESTON. Pardon me. Senator Rubio, I believe that the administration has pursued a policy of being as transparent on matters of national security as national security will permit. In this particular area, I think that we have been very clear in stating, for the Congress and publicly, where it is that U.S. forces are using military force under the AUMF, against whom, and on what basis.

My prepared statement, my oral statement today, it clearly states the groups against which the United States is currently operating and which the United States military is currently applying military force under the authority of the AUMF.

Senator RUBIO. I guess—the reason why I am asking that question is because the nature of al-Qaeda has changed since the AUMF was first passed. It has spread to different places. As I understand what you have said here today, the administration has not taken a position as to whether the existing AUMF should be expanded or revised to take into account the changing nature of the threat.

Mr. PRESTON. Well, the President has made very clear that he would not support expanding the existing AUMF, but he has also made very clear that he fully supports the effort to examine the AUMF toward its refinement to ensure that it is narrowly tailored to meet that evolving threat.

Senator RUBIO. Does he not support expanding the AUMF because he believes he does not need that authority, he already has it, or is it because he simply wants to bring to an end this conflict and he believes that the war against al-Qaeda is winding up?

Mr. PRESTON. I think he has explained it in terms of wanting authority toward a series of persistent, targeted efforts to dismantle specific networks of violent extremists that threaten our country and getting away from a regime in which there is unbound powers more suited for judicial armed conflict between nation-states. So, I think that——

Senator RUBIO. But, I guess the problem that I have is, I am trying to understand, Is it because he believes that the existing authorities he now has—because al-Qaeda continues to evolve and find new havens in which to operate from, and we cannot necessarily predict where that is, 10 years out, 5 years out, 3 years out. So, what I am trying to understand, from a legal perspective, is, Is it his believe that, under his inherent powers as Commander in Chief, he does not need the authority of the Congress to go after that in—or—and therefore, that is why we no longer need to expand the AUMF, or revise it to account for that new threat?

Mr. PRESTON. Sir, I think his beliefs are best stated in his public statements, and, most particularly, the NDU speech and the State of the Union. What——

Senator RUBIO. Which State of the Union? Because in one State of the Union, he said that al-Qaeda was on the run and that—basically, he made it sound like that they were incapable of posing an ongoing threat. I think now he would not say that, today, given the realities that we have now seen emerge.

Mr. PRESTON. Well, I was referring to the most recent State of the Union. But, my point is that we are engaged in an effort at addressing precisely the questions that you are posing, in terms of what future legal framework is best suited to adequately meet the terrorist threat as it has evolved, and narrowly tailored to meet that threat, and not granting unbound powers of all-out warfighting of the sort you get between nation-states.

Senator RUBIO. But, going back to this analogy that you are using, of nation-states, it is, in fact, a reality, in the 21st century, that—one of the challenges we have is that these most dangerous conflicts that we now find ourself in are not against nation-states, they are against nonstate actors who do not necessarily have the confines of a nation-state, but they present a very serious risk to the United States. And so, I guess my problem with the terminology that you keep using, in terms of pulling us away from conflicts that may look like the ones we once had against nation-states, is that, in essence, that is the modern threat, is these—in addition to nation-states that pose a threat, are these nonstate actors that are a very serious threat.

But, I want to pivot back to another point that I know is of interest to some members of the committee, and that is the following. We have seen open-source reporting in evidence, for example, that in Syria there are a large number of foreign fighters, including many Westerners. And I read an open-source reporting article today that estimated that as many as 100 Americans may be involved with jihadist groups within Syria. What authorities does the United States have to target individual American—even if they happen to be American citizens who are affiliated with radical groups such as these and are actively participating in their efforts to target America and America's interests?

Ms. McLEOD. Senator Rubio, the United States has the authority to target individuals, including Americans, who pose an imminent threat of armed attack to our country. And it is, of course, a very grave matter to decide to use lethal force against a U.S. citizen, but, in some cases, it has proven to be necessary.

Senator RUBIO. Ms. McLeod, I wanted to ask you, actually—in your view, and in the view of the State Department, is al-Qaeda and its affiliates today—are they a widespread threat against America or are they a targeted threat against America? Are they just isolated groups that from time to time are problematic, or is this part of a larger growing, evolving problem that, quite frankly, at this stage, is unpredictable but seems to trend toward growth?

Ms. McLEOD. I think it is fair to say, as I believe the President said in his NDU speech, that, while core al-Qaeda has been gravely diminished, there is an evolving threat with respect to affiliates of al-Qaeda who are located in various parts of the world.

Senator RUBIO. Is it not fair to say that, instead of one core al-Qaeda, we now see emerging eight or nine core al-Qaedas, just because they are now dispersed into different areas? And, in addition to al-Qaeda, by the way, they are not the only radical Islamic threat that the West faces—al-Qaeda in—as we define it. There are also other radical groups out there that we know pose a threat to American interests around the world, and even potentially in the homeland, right?

Ms. McLEOD. Yes, that is correct. And I believe—and some of those would not be covered by the AUMF. But, as I believe we said, we believe the President has authority to proceed against those groups if they, indeed——

Senator RUBIO. So, just to understand the position, there are additional groups, outside of the Taliban and al-Qaeda, that pose a serious threat to our national security, they are not covered under the AUMF, but you do not believe that we need to revise the AUMF to cover them, because you have existing constitutional authorities that allow you to target them if, in fact, they pose that threat.

Ms. McLEOD. I did not say that we have determined that there are other groups that pose an imminent threat to the United States. I said we would have the authority to proceed against them if we, indeed, made those determinations.

Senator RUBIO. Without an AUMF expansion.

Ms. McLEOD. Yes.

The CHAIRMAN. Senator Johnson.

Senator JOHNSON. Thank you, Mr. Chair.

I am finding this hearing quite confusing. I mean, it is true that, on May 23, 2013, President Obama did declare the global war on terror over? That is a correct statement, true? Does he believe that? I mean, you are working in this administration. Do you believe President Obama believes the global war on terror is over?

Mr. PRESTON. Well, I guess I would just point out—I believe the view of the administration is that we are engaged in armed conflict. We are engaged in armed conflict with al-Qaeda, with the Taliban, and with associated forces. That conflict continues.

Senator JOHNSON. So, really, nobody in the administration really believes the global war on terror is over. I mean, we are still involved in conflict.

Mr. PRESTON. I think the administration has not embraced the characterization of a global war on terror as if the enemy here were a religion or a set of techniques——

Senator JOHNSON. So, it is just—semantically, we are not in a global war on terror, we are just in a war against terrorist elements. Is that the——

Mr. PRESTON. We are at war with al-Qaeda, the Taliban, and associated forces, and we are actively involved in efforts to detect and address threats from terrorist elements otherwise.

Senator JOHNSON. Do you believe the AUMF covered the current situation?

Mr. PRESTON. I think the AUMF has served well in providing full authority to use military force against our enemies in those conflicts.

Senator JOHNSON. So, why would the administration not have a position of whether or not they want the AUMF to continue or they want it repealed?

Mr. PRESTON. I think the administration, through the President, almost a year ago, has clearly stated a policy favoring refinement and, ultimately, repeal of the statute. That, I do not think translates into, necessarily, immediate repeal of the statute.

Senator JOHNSON. So, has the administration proposed any refinement or any redefinition of the AUMF? I mean, have they provided us language, in terms of what they think they need to handle the current situation?

Ms. McLEOD. No, Senator. We have not. We need to engage with you all to get your ideas and take them back. And we are actively——

Senator JOHNSON. Well, like Senator Kaine said, this is engagement. Why would you not lay down a proposal so we could evaluate it? I mean, why will the administration not—as President of the United States, I mean, he is in charge of foreign policy. He is the Commander in Chief. Why would he not bring us the language he needs to prosecute this evolving war on terror? I mean, that is what I would like to see. I do not think it is my job. I am not an attorney, I do not understand the complexity of these things. I would like to see the administration propose what it needs in a refined Authorization of Use for Military Force.

The CHAIRMAN. Senator Johnson, if I might add, you know, it seems that the President, in May, established an objective, if you will, the repeal and—the refinement and, ultimately, the repeal. He has set us about a course to focus on and develop a future legal framework for the use of force.

Senator JOHNSON. Okay. Oh, good, good. So, we are on a course.

Is he going to provide any kind of roadmap, in terms of what he needs? He is the Commander in Chief. He is the one that needs the authorization. Is he going to come to Congress and let us know what he needs to stay within his constitutional powers to protect this Nation? Is he going to provide a proposal that we can review and that we can debate? Or are we supposed to come up with one? I mean, what is the process going to be?

Mr. PRESTON. I think, as he said, in May have last year, that he envisions the administration's engaging with Congress, with this and other——

Senator JOHNSON. That was a year ago.

Mr. PRESTON. I understand that.

Senator JOHNSON. He declared the war on terror over, and now we are having a hearing, and there is no proposal, there is no language, there is really nothing, that I am hearing in this setting, in terms of what he wants, what he needs. When are we going to get that? How do we get to that point? Where does the engagement actually occur, then?

Mr. PRESTON. The way I would describe it, sir, is that he has established an objective, a vision, if you will, that we formulate a post-Iraq and -Afghanistan legal framework. He is——

Senator JOHNSON. So, who is going to do that?

Mr. PRESTON. He did not establish that as an immediate tasking, but as something that we need to take on deliberately and at the—and then engage with Congress——

Senator JOHNSON. So, why did he declare the war on terror over, a year ago? I mean, again, this makes no sense to me.

Can you—again, I am not an attorney, I am relatively new to this process, here—can you define an "imminent threat"? I mean, if we would do away with the AUMF, if we did not have one on the books—and I believe that the President does have the authority to protect this Nation—what is an "imminent threat"? Can you explain that, in layman's terms? How is that made operational?

Ms. MCLEOD. Senator Johnson, most obviously an individual who is planning a specific attack against U.S. persons would be an "imminent threat" against the United States. And a person that is hard to articulate all of the factors that would go into a decision of whether an individual poses an imminent threat, but I want to read to you from what the Attorney General said in explaining this concept, because the Justice Department has done some long and hard thinking on this.

And he explained that the determination of whether an individual presents an imminent threat may incorporate consideration of the relevant window of opportunity to act against that individual, the possible harm that missing the window could create, and the likelihood of heading off further disastrous attacks against the United States. And then he said, with respect to the kind of terrorist threat that we are facing today, "We learned, on 9/11, that al-Qaeda has demonstrated the ability to strike with little or no notice, and to cause devastating casualties. Its leaders are continually planning attacks against the United States, and they do not behave like a traditional military, wearing uniforms, carrying arms openly, or amassing forces in preparation for an attack. Given these facts, the Constitution does not require the President to delay action until some theoretical end stage of planning when the precise time, place, and manner of an attack become clear. Such a requirement would create an unacceptably high risk that our efforts would fail and that Americans would be''——

Senator JOHNSON. Okay, listen. I completely understand this is an amorphous, evolving, incredibly difficult threat. And I realize the standards are quite amorphous, as well. I guess what I am asking for is that the administration—this President lead, that he comes and proposes to us what language, you know, what he needs to actually carry out his constitutional duty of protecting this Nation. That would be the way I would like to see this administration engage with us.

Thank you, Mr. Chairman.

Ms. McLeod. Senator, we will certainly take that back.

The Chairman. Let me just, before I call the next member— I think, in fairness to these witnesses, policy is not their purview. Legal analysis is. And it is in that context that I invited these witnesses to appear before the committee, to get a legal analysis of the issues that surround the President and any potential AUMF. Members, of course, are free to pursue policy discussions. But, if I wanted to hear the policy of the administration today, I probably would have invited a different set of witnesses.

Senator Corker. Since that comment was made——

The Chairman. And I may do that in the future.

Senator Corker. Okay. I would just like to say, though, the fact is that what the witnesses have said is, they do not know what current operations rely on the AUMF. That is what they have said. So, in fairness, they may not be speaking to policy, but they cannot even answer a question as to what operations rely on what authorities. So——

The Chairman. Well, I am referring to the broader questions that have been raised here about, What does the administration view as the AUMF that they would desire? I do not think that that is in the bailiwick of the witnesses before us. In that context.

But, Senator Murphy has deferred, for the moment. So, Senator Flake, you are up next. And you are going to defer to Senator McCain.

Senator McCain.

Senator McCain. Thank you.

And I appreciate the deference that Senator Flake gives to me, and I am sure it will be short-lived over time. [Laughter.]

I thank you, Mr. Chairman, and I thank my friend.

Mr. Preston, in testimony in the Senate Armed Services Committee, the Director of National Intelligence, James Clapper, and the Director of the DIA, agreed that al-Qaeda and its associated forces are not on the run and not on a path to defeat. Subsequent testimony in the Armed Services Committee, General Austin, General Rodriguez, and others, stated that the threat posed by al-Qaeda and its associated forces is increasing, not decreasing, in their geographic areas of responsibilities.

Do you agree with our senior military and intelligence leaders, that al-Qaeda and its associated forces have not been defeated?

Mr. Preston. As General Counsel——

Senator McCain. You know, it is a fairly straightforward question. Do you agree that—with our senior military and intelligence——

Mr. Preston. My lane is the law, so I would defer to the senior intelligence and military——

Senator McCain. So, you do not want to answer.

Mr. Preston [continuing]. On matters of intelligence and operations.

Senator MCCAIN. I see. Working over at the Department of Defense, you would not have a view of that, even though you told this committee, at your confirmation, that you would answer questions, if asked.

Mr. PRESTON. I would just——

Senator MCCAIN. In your personal opinion, do you think that the DOD counterterrorism operations, and those that conduct them, are better served by maintaining the 2001 AUMF unchanged, repealing, or updating it in some way, Mr. Preston?

Mr. PRESTON. Senator McCain, that is precisely the set of issues that we agency lawyers in the administration are focused on and that the President, I think, has foretold engaging with Congress on.

Senator MCCAIN. Again, a nonanswer. So, according to your answers to previous questions, either with or without AUMF authority, the United States can attack those that pose a imminent threat to the United States of America. Is that correct?

Mr. PRESTON. I believe the legal authority is there, yes, sir.

Senator MCCAIN. I see. And would you say that the people who attacked our Embassy—our consulate in Benghazi are a terrorist organization?

Mr. PRESTON. I understand that they are, yes, sir.

Senator MCCAIN. So, therefore, would we have the authority to strike, with a drone, members of that organization that attacked our consulate and killed four Americans?

Mr. PRESTON. I think, if and when a concrete situation is presented, the judgment is that that group presents the requisite threat, then there is that authority. Or if that group is determined to fall within the AUMF, there would be that authority.

Senator MCCAIN. So, you just agreed that they were part of a terrorist organization, right?

Mr. PRESTON. Yes, sir.

Senator MCCAIN. So, if they are part of a terrorist organization, according to the interpretation of the AUMF, then is it your view the President has the authority to attack them and eliminate them?

Mr. PRESTON. I think there are multiple potential sources of——

Senator MCCAIN. I am asking, in your view, does the President, under the AUMF and the authorities that you say he has, do they have a legal right to strike members of the organization that committed the attack on Benghazi?

Mr. PRESTON. There is the authority to use military force if they present an imminent threat and/or if they qualify as an associated force of al-Qaeda. So, the answer——

Senator MCCAIN. I just asked you if they did, and you said yes.

Mr. PRESTON. Well, sir, that depends on the particular factual circumstances, and it is a judgment that is made on that basis. But, the answer——

Senator MCCAIN. Whew.

Mr. PRESTON. I think the short answer is that our government is committed to applying all lawfully available instruments of national power. That includes law enforcement authority——

Senator MCCAIN. I am asking, specifically, about a situation where four Americans were killed, that was carried out by a terrorist organization—that has been the conclusion—whether the

President of the United States, in your legal opinion, has the authority to strike these people and eliminate them. Now, that is a pretty straightforward question.

Mr. PRESTON. And I think I have tried to answer it as straightforwardly——

Senator MCCAIN. Then the answer is "yes" or "no." Does he have the authority, or not?

Mr. PRESTON. I believe——

Senator MCCAIN. You are not being straightforward, sir.

Mr. PRESTON. There are two sources of authority, and——

Senator MCCAIN. I am asking whether he has the authority, not the sources of authority.

Mr. PRESTON. And that requires a determination as to——

Senator MCCAIN. That is a third nonanswer. Nicely done. You are——

Mr. PRESTON. I have tried my best.

Senator MCCAIN. It is remarkable.

So, does the—the President said he wants to refine and, ultimately, repeal the AUMF's mandate. That was his speech at the—President's speech in the National Defense University. Does that mean that, if the AUMF were repealed, that that would mean that the detention facility at Guantanamo would be, then, closed?

Mr. PRESTON. I think that is a critical issue that is in the mix, inasmuch as the AUMF is a domestic source of authority for——

Senator MCCAIN. I am asking, again, Does that mean that the detention facility at Guantanamo would then required to be closed if the AUMF were, as the President desires, ultimately repealed?

Mr. PRESTON. It would create a substantial question about our ability to do long-term detention, which is what is going on at the Guantanamo facility.

Senator MCCAIN. I am wasting the committee's time.

The CHAIRMAN. Senator Murphy.

Senator MURPHY. Thank you very much, Mr. Chairman.

This morning, I have, unfortunately, missed part of the hearing. I was under the wonderful care of a constituent of Senator Kaine's, getting a root canal. And it sounds like the experience of the witnesses and perhaps some members of this committee may have been more or less pleasant than mine—experience this morning. But, I am glad to be here.

And what has been explained to me is that the panel has given a pretty robust defense of the administration's Article 2 powers. And I guess if I was sitting in your seat, I would probably do the same, or some version of the same, with maybe some more specific answers as to the hypotheticals that were, I think, pretty clear to be posed today.

So, let me ask you a broader question. I think there is a reason why it is Article 2 that lays out the administration's powers, and not Article 1. I think there is a reason why we are all subject to Article 1, and there are very specific powers given to Congress with respect to foreign affairs in Article 1: the power to declare war and the power to raise armies.

And so, I am just going to ask you—you are both lawyers, you both have studied both articles well—I am just going to ask a very broad question, which is, In your mind, where does Article 2 powers end and Article 1 powers begin? What is your rendering of what is left in Article 1 if we understand the broad rendering of Article 2 powers that you have explained today? Tell us what— instead of explaining what your role is, let me flip it. Explain to us what our role is.

Mr. PRESTON. Senator, let me start with a very general proposition, which is the strongly held belief that our government works best, and our Nation is strongest, in matters of military force and war, when both of the political branches are working together. So, the short, and perhaps most important, answer is, both Congress and the Executive need, and ought, to work together on matters of military force and war.

Beyond that, it is, I think, very much a part of the President's initiative, in May at the NDU speech, in inviting dialogue with Congress to ensure that the administration is engaging with Congress as we seek to develop that future legal framework.

Congress obviously enacted the 2001 AUMF and provided the congressional imprimatur for the use of force in that setting, and we very much look forward to engaging with Congress as we seek to shape what that follow-on or future legal framework will look like.

Senator MURPHY. Ms. McLeod.

Ms. McLEOD. Senator Murphy, I do not think I am going to be able, even though I am a lawyer, to give you a precise delineation of authority between the Congress and the executive branch in the area of the use of military force. I think this has been the subject of much debate in the scholarly world, and I think that the War Powers Resolution was enacted to try and achieve a mechanism under which we could consult with the Congress before using force, and provide reporting, and, if necessary, get authorization.

Senator MURPHY. You clearly believe that if an individual has made a threat against the United States and is carrying it out, you have existing authority, with or without the AUMF, to pursue that individual. Correct?

Ms. McLEOD. If they pose an imminent threat, yes. But, I would point out, there are other constraints that can come into play. If that individual is in a different country, there are certain considerations of sovereignty that we have to address. So, you have to consider whether you can get consent; or, if not, you have to consider whether that country is unable or unwilling to address the threat to us, in which case we would still feel we were able to——

Senator MURPHY. But, those are considerations separate and aside from whether or not you need consent from Congress.

Ms. McLEOD. Yes.

Senator MURPHY. If an organization has, in your mind, constituted an imminent threat, is there any limitation on the size of that organization that would require you to come to the Congress, so long as you had made a determination that they posed an imminent threat?

Ms. McLEOD. No, I do not—I do not think so.

Senator MURPHY. A nation harboring an entity that poses an imminent threat, in coordination with that entity that poses an imminent threat, if that country has not, itself, expressed a threat to the United States, but is harboring an entity or organization that poses an imminent threat, in order to pursue conduct against that nation, do you need prior congressional authorization?

Ms. McLEOD. Well, I would say that our actions taken in self-defense always have to be necessary and proportionate. So, we would have to go through that analysis before considering what action, if any, we could take against a state that harbored terrorists. And we would have to consider—I think I am—we would have to think about whether that—whether individuals in that state were—or the government of that state—actually posed an imminent threat.

Senator MURPHY. And there would not necessarily be a time limitation on it.

So, let me get this straight. So, you are suggesting that the state, itself, would have to pose an imminent threat, not simply harboring or providing or hosting an organization that provides an imminent threat.

Ms. McLEOD. I think I need to think about your question further. I cannot give you a definitive answer.

Senator MURPHY. I will—and my line of questioning there—I mean, to the extent that we—I will express the same level of frustration that others on the panel have faced here to—that is a critical question—in part, because, you know, we have dealt with that question in real terms over the last decade. We had a nation that harbored a terrorist group that, arguably, did not present an independent threat to the United States. In that case, there was an authorization of military force.

But, a suggestion that the Executive can undertake an action against a sovereign, independent nation simply because they have made a decision to harbor that organization, and not have to come to the United States Congress, with war-making authorities, for that authorization, that is—I would love a clear "no" to that question. I would love a clear indication that, if a nation has not presented an imminent threat and is simply harboring an organization, that, in order to wage war against a sovereign nation, you would have to come to the United States Congress for authorization.

Ms. McLEOD. Senator, I would note that we did just that in seeking——

Senator MURPHY. I understand you did, but to the—but, it would be nice to hear, very clearly, that your interpretation of the law is that you are always required, in that circumstance, to come to the Congress.

Thank you.

The CHAIRMAN. Senator Flake.

Senator FLAKE. Thank you.

I planned, but I believe it was already asked by Senator Corker, just, in the absence of—if the AUMF were to sunset tomorrow, what advice would you give to the President, in terms of what activities we are involved in around the world that we would need to cease. And I understand that you are—you say that—none of them, that you would not offer any advice to disengage or to not continue anything that is being done. Is that——

Mr. PRESTON. I think, Senator, what I would say is that the impact of that on operations in Afghanistan, against al-Qaeda elsewhere, detention operations—those are all things that we would need to examine in framing whatever future follow-on legal framework would be in place.

The point we were making earlier is that, on the fundamental question of authority to take military action in order to address and protect the country from imminent threat of armed attack, that that authority does exist in the Constitution with the President, quite apart from the presence of a legislative authorization.

Senator FLAKE. There has been quite a bit of talk of hypotheticals, here, what would happen here or there. Why do we not take an actual case, here. And I would like your explanation as to where the President got his authority.

Let us take Libya. In the spring of 2011, was Libya a sovereign country?

Ms. McLEOD. Yes, it was.

Senator FLAKE. Was there an imminent threat posed to the United States?

Ms. McLEOD. In the case of Libya, the U.S. took military action as a matter of international law, pursuant to an authorization by the U.N. Security Council, which has authority to take measures that are binding on states or can give authority to states to take action in order to address threats to peace and security.

Senator FLAKE. So, not pursuant to any AUMF here. But, we took military action that was not under the auspices of the United Nations, though.

Ms. McLEOD. No, it was not under the auspices, per se, but the Security Council resolutions specifically authorized NATO and others to take the military action.

Senator FLAKE. We took military action, though, independent of the United Nations, on our own. We put Osprey aircraft there, we needed to rescue a pilot later. So, this was not action that was pursuant to a U.N. Security Council resolution, was it not? This is action that we took independently, still.

Ms. McLEOD. I believe it was pursuant to the U.N. Security Council resolution, Senator.

Senator FLAKE. But, right now we are moving troops to Italy to be closer to the situation in Libya. If we were to move in, what auspices would we be moving in now? I think we hear reports that four additional Osprey aircraft arrived overnight in Italy to join four B–52s and 200 marines that had been moved there last week. Libya, things are going south there pretty quickly. If we were to move into Libya and take some action there, would it be under— under what authority would it be?

Ms. McLEOD. Senator, I believe the troops that are in Italy are being positioned there in case our personnel at the U.S. Embassy need to be evacuated, which is a very standard——

Senator FLAKE. Certainly.

Ms. McLEOD [continuing]. Operation that we——

Senator FLAKE. Nobody would argue with that. But, additional action that was taken—that would be taken would—would it be pursuant to some U.N. Security Council resolution or under the President's Article 2 powers or—certainly not under any AUMF that has been passed here.

Ms. McLEOD. Well, I am not aware that any sort of military action, beyond the possibility of going in and extracting our personnel, has been under discussion.

Senator FLAKE. All right.

Well, I said I share the frustration that others here have expressed that we were told that an additional—you know, that the President would like to refine the AUMF, and ultimately eliminate it. But, when asked what would change if the AUMF were absent tomorrow and we did not have it, then we do not get much of answer on what would change, in terms of any activities we are involved with now. So, it leaves Congress with not much direction from the administration as to what the administration really wants, here. So, it is just—it is a bit confusing.

Thank you.

The CHAIRMAN. Let me—I have a couple of other questions, and there may be one or two members who have some—let me—look, I think part of our challenge, here, is that this area of the law is not fully defined. And so, that is—at least from my perspective—so, I think that is part of the challenge. But, I do want to clarify some things, or at least understand clearly, for the record, where you stand.

In pursuance of Senator Flake's questions, our action in Libya was a humanitarian action, in a sense, maybe subject to, you know, a NATO action and maybe subject to some Security Council resolutions, but does it—is it your opinion that those authorizations of a NATO operation or a Security Council resolution allows a President, who is not responding to imminent threat, to circumvent the United States Congress, in terms of an authorization for the use of force? Because that is basically what I heard you say. And if I am wrong about understanding what you said, please correct me.

Ms. McLEOD. No, Senator, that was not what I was saying.

The CHAIRMAN. Okay.

Ms. McLEOD. I was talking about——

The CHAIRMAN. What did you say?

Ms. McLEOD [continuing]. International law authority for us to use force in that case.

The CHAIRMAN. But, in international law authority to use force, that is what gives you the imprimatur to go act against a certain country. But, to use the forces of the United States even under that international law, would you not have to come to the Congress to get authorization to act? Especially when it is not an imminent-threat situation.

Ms. McLEOD. In the case of Libya, we did file a report, if not more than one report, under the War Powers Resolution, and we consulted with the Congress on the actions we were taking.

The CHAIRMAN. The——

Ms. McLEOD. But, it is true, we did not seek prior authorization.

The CHAIRMAN. Yes. And even under the War Powers Act, of course, there would be an action by the President, but, within a certain time period, there would have to be a response from the Congress. I am concerned, while I believe in Security Council resolutions to create international support in efforts and direction to intervene in the sovereignty of another country, I am still am concerned that, when we want to participate under such an umbrella, that there must be an authorization of the Congress to do so if it is not an imminent-threat situation.

So, I would like you to all go rethink that and come back at some point, either you or policymakers, to define for us what your view is. It may not be my view, but I would like to hear what your view is.

Let me ask you, Did the President need the authorization for the use of force, had he decided to act in the chemical weapons issue in Syria?

[Pause.]

Ms. McLEOD. As you know, the President ultimately did decide that he would seek congressional authorization.

The CHAIRMAN. I know he did. But, my question is, Did he need to do that, or do you believe he had the authorities, based upon what had transpired in Syria with Assad using chemical weapons against his people? Did he need authority, or did he not need authority? Did he have the authority to act, independent of the Congress?

Ms. McLEOD. Senator, it would be my view, but I—mine was not—I was not the one who made this decision. It would be my view that he would have the authority to act, but that it was prudent, as he did, to seek the authorization——

The CHAIRMAN. You believe he had the authority act, notwithstanding.

Now, that is not, per se, an imminent threat to the United States, as far as I can tell. It is certainly something I strongly supported giving the President the power for, as did most of the members of this committee. But, there was no indication, at least to my knowledge, that those chemical weapons would be used against U.S. citizens, U.S. forces, or whatnot. So, this is where we need to define what is the standard.

Let me ask you a third question. And you can divvy up your responses, as may be appropriate, between your two respective roles.

The United States plans to end its combat operations in Afghanistan by the end of the year. While the 2001 AUMF has been the primary basis in domestic law authorizing these operations, its authorization is not limited to operations in Afghanistan. Nevertheless, the end of combat operations in Afghanistan, and the absence of sustained combat operations under the 2001 AUMF in any other theater, will undoubtedly have implications for the continued use of this authority in other contexts. So, could you please describe for the committee what you anticipate to be the consequences, in terms of the limits of legal authority, of the end of Afghanistan combat operations in the following three areas: one, detention operations at Guantanamo Bay in Cuba; two, targeted killing operations against al-Qaeda and associated forces; and three, Defense Department counterterrorism operations, including relevant security assistance?

Mr. PRESTON. Let me tackle that one, Mr. Chairman.

The CHAIRMAN. Okay.

Mr. PRESTON. Ms. McLeod can supplement, as appropriate. And let me address that, first, generally, and then specifically the areas you mentioned.

The President has made clear that it is not in our national interest to remain on a perpetual wartime footing, and that this war, like all others, will come to an end. At the same time, while the United States military mission in Afghanistan, after 2014, is an important milestone, it does not necessarily mark the end of the armed conflict with the Taliban. Now, of course, as we seek to finalize what precisely the presence and mission in Afghanistan will be, we would better able to judge its impact on that armed conflict.

By similar token, even when the conflict with the Taliban ends, that will not necessarily mark the end of the conflict with al-Qaeda. And it is in that context that we look at the three issues that you raised.

First, I believe, was detention. The United States will continue to have legal authority to detain individuals from al-Qaeda, the Taliban, associated forces, until the end of the armed conflict, as a matter of international law and, as we have discussed earlier, under the AUMF.

In terms of the targeted strikes that you were referring to—and I would say, more broadly, direct action against counterterrorism targets, which would include capture operations or lethal operations—again, while the United States mission in Afghanistan is a—in its narrowing post-2014 is an important consideration—we will retain the authority to use force, as appropriate, against our enemies in the armed conflict and otherwise to protect to the country.

The third area that you mentioned is foreign assistance or other counterterrorism activities and assistance. And that, again, notwithstanding the narrowing of the mission in Afghanistan, we would expect that DOD's assistance efforts—and, in particular, capacity-building by partner countries—will continue apace and unabated.

The CHAIRMAN. So, your answer, then, to my three specific questions is that you will have continuing legal authority, notwithstanding the ending of that conflict or any narrowing or repealing of the AUMF under which you are operating in Afghanistan.

Mr. PRESTON. I agree with most of what you said, sir. With the end of the conflict—and we do face issues about—under international law principles—the extent to which use of force in certain applications would continue to be justified under international law.

The CHAIRMAN. Let me say one final thing and then I will turn to Senator Corker.

Would it be fair to say that statutory authorization essentially provides a broader authority on which to act militarily, particularly in the absence of an immediate threat?

Mr. PRESTON. It certainly can. And in the case of the AUMF, it does represent a broad grant of authority.

The CHAIRMAN. And an AUMF also transcends the War Power Resolution, because it requires the President to come to Congress for authorization 30 days after insertion of U.S. forces in hostilities.

Mr. PRESTON. That is right. A legislated authorization provides Congress' participation in that decision.

The CHAIRMAN. Senator Corker.

Senator CORKER. Mr. Chairman, I will be very brief. I do want to thank you for having this hearing. I think it is been very educational for all involved, even though it has been difficult to get direct answers. I think it has really highlighted, in many ways, a real debate that needs to occur here in action taken by the committee.

I do want to say, for my friends who may not have been here during the Libya debate—I know that Harold Koh is here and will be a witness in just a moment. I know sometimes people leave these hearings. But, when we challenged the administration over the War Powers Act issue as we were bombing Libya—bombing Libya—Mr. Koh testified, on behalf of the State Department, that we were not involved in hostilities in Libya.

So, I just want to highlight the fact that this is a real debate that we need to have. There are people who, on behalf of the administration, want to give any answer that works for the administration, will justify actions that, to me, go beyond. And so, I really want to thank you so much for having this debate.

And I would like to ask Mr. Preston which of these groups—I am going to name some groups—you are authorized to go after under the 9/11 AUMF.

AQAP, yes or no?

Mr. PRESTON. As I said in my statement, we have previously disclosed that AQAP is a part of or——

Senator CORKER. Is it yes—I want to move through this quickly. Yes or no?

Mr. PRESTON. It—yes, sir.

Senator CORKER. ISIS?

Mr. PRESTON. Sir, with respect to groups in addition to the ones that——

Senator CORKER. Yes or no? I want a yes-or-no answer. Are you authorized, under the 9/11 AUMF, to go after ISIS?

Mr. PRESTON. Sir, I cannot speak publicly about which groups—particular groups we may or may not have determined——

Senator CORKER. Is this a classified answer? Is that the reason?

Mr. PRESTON. That is my understanding, yes, sir.

Senator CORKER. So, I do wonder how—again, this gets back to a topic many of us discussed last night—I do not know how we can debate these issues, when you cannot even tell us whether we can or cannot go after groups based on authorizations that Congress itself passed. I just want to highlight that.

AQIM. Can we go after AQIM? Yes——

Mr. PRESTON. Same answer——

Senator CORKER [continuing]. Or no?

Mr. PRESTON [continuing]. Sir——

Senator CORKER. Same answer. Classified, you cannot tell us——

Mr. PRESTON. We would——

Senator CORKER [continuing]. Whether we can go after groups in northern Africa that are committing——

Mr. PRESTON. We have publicly identified the groups that we are operating against using military force under AUMF. As for other groups, whether or not they would qualify is a determination that is made as concrete situations are presented.

Senator CORKER. Well, there are very concrete situations happening. So, right now, you have made a determination, I guess, with ISIS. Very concrete things are happening there in AQIM. So,

I assume, in a classified setting, you could share with us whether, in fact, you have the authorities to go after these groups. Is that correct?

Mr. PRESTON. In a classified setting, we could discuss the available classified intelligence and how the standards——

Senator CORKER. No, I just want to know if we can or cannot. Can you tell me those things in a classified setting?

Mr. PRESTON. That would have to take place in a classified setting.

Senator CORKER. Okay. Well, I will set that up the first day we are back, and I look forward to that meeting.

Al-Nusra.

Mr. PRESTON. Sir, again, the groups that we have not identified as groups we are currently operating against, the intelligence and application of the standards under the AUMF is not something that we are prepared to discuss in an open session.

Senator CORKER. But, in a classified setting, you will share that with the entire committee.

Mr. PRESTON. That would have to take place in a classified setting.

Senator CORKER. Well, since we—I just will close with this. Ms. McLeod, I know I gave you somewhat of a hard time, and I know that you are sent up here on behalf of the State Department to represent the State Department. And I actually want to say to you that my wrath should really be taken toward the State Department and not yourself. We asked people to come up here today to answer questions that I think are of a great challenge for our Nation to deal with. And just as Ann Patterson came up here 56 days ago and told us that she would be glad to lay out to us what our policy was in Syria, it has never happened. I think you all know.

And I realized, actually, last night, while the administration has been hiding behind intelligence, not being able to share it—I realized, last night, that the administration has no policy in Syria, has no strategy in Syria, and that is why they have not been willing to talk with us about this. It just dawned on me last night why this stonewalling is taking place. There is no objective there other than acting like we are doing something.

And I just want to say to this group, it is obvious the administration has no opinion—has no opinion—on whether we should refine the AUMF, or not.

And I just want to say to Chad, who works on behalf of the State Department, you would serve the State Department much better by actually sending folks up here who can speak to these issues, or just tell us that there is no opinion that the State Department has.

And so, with that, I thank you both for being here. I apologize, on behalf of the Departments you represent, them sending you up here, when they really do not have, quote—as the Chairman referenced appropriately, they have not made any policy statements.

I do hope the committee will take this issue up. And again, I want to thank the chairman for his diligence. My guess is—this has peaked a lot of interest here, and my guess is that if we are going to be responsible Senators, we should respond.

The CHAIRMAN. Senator Durbin.

Senator DURBIN. Very briefly, because I know there is another panel.

I do not know that there were any Members of the Senate who really understood, when we voted on this Authorization for the Use of Military Force, what we were voting for. We were reacting to the 9/11 attack and saying, ''Go after those responsible.'' None of us could have envisioned that we were voting for the longest war in the history of the United States, which still goes on, to this day. None of us could have understood the military aspects and non-military aspects of the commitment that we were making. And I think it is entirely appropriate, though monumentally challenging, for us to take on a redefinition of the Authorization of the Use of Military Force.

And I would say to my friend—and he is my friend—Senator Corker, of Tennessee—his frustration over this reflects many things, not the least of which are the rules of the Senate about how information is exchanged and given to Members of the Senate. As I mentioned to him last night in a separate meeting, in a separate capacity from this committee, I am told things that other Members are not. And I understand when witnesses come before us and say, ''I—you know, I am dutybound not to disclose classified information in an open public hearing. It may endanger lives of Americans and others.'' That is a responsibility that I am sure you take very seriously. And I would not put you on the spot as to whether or not any specific piece of information—your right to make that claim. But, I do believe we need to discuss, as an institution, the exchange of more information so that we understand the nature of this conflict we are now in with terrorism. It is much different than any of us envisioned when we were voting that day on the Authorization of the Use of Military Force.

Thank you, Mr. Chairman.

Mr. PRESTON. Sir, if I could just thank Senator Durbin for those comments, and particularly about the information. We will take back Senator Corker's request for additional information that I am not at liberty to provide.

Thank you.

The CHAIRMAN. Is there any other member who has any questions? [No response.]

If not, with the appreciation of the committee, this panel is excused.

Let me call up our next panel, a very important panel: The Honorable Harold Koh, Sterling Professor of International Law, Yale Law School, and former State Department Legal Adviser; and the Honorable Michael Mukasey, partner, Debevoise & Plimpton, former Attorney General of the United States.

I welcome both of you to the committee. We appreciate your willingness to share your insights. Your full statements are going to be included in the record, without objection. So, I would ask you to try to summarize them in about 5 minutes or so. And this way, we can get into the type of dialogue that we just had with the previous panel.

And, with that, Mr. Koh, you are recognized.

STATEMENT OF HON. HAROLD HONGJU KOH, STERLING PROFESSOR OF INTERNATIONAL LAW, YALE LAW SCHOOL, FORMER STATE DEPARTMENT LEGAL ADVISER, NEW HAVEN, CT

Mr. KOH. Thank you, Mr. Chair, Ranking Member Corker, for inviting me back.

A year ago, the President gave a speech, at the National Defense University, that outlined elements of his post-9/11 counterterrorism strategy. And there are three aspects that I think are particularly important and achievable, which I have described in my written statement: First, eventually ending the war with al-Qaeda and the associated forces when the facts on the ground permit. And that is the key. The nature of the threat on the ground is what matters and is logically prior to any legal action. Second, eventually repealing the AUMF. And third, in the meantime, narrowing its mandate.

And, to me, each of these three elements—ending the war with al-Qaeda, seeking repeal, and narrowing the AUMF—is possible, in time. So, there are three questions to which each—the answer, I think, should be "yes."

Should our long-term goal be ending the war? Yes. I think we should choose an exit strategy over a perpetual war, because war has a distorting effect on our priorities, our economies, and our liberties. And, under our Constitution, peace is the norm; perpetual war is a distortion.

And I do not think that Congress should extend or expand the war, over the President's objection. First of all, it is Congress' role to end wars. And, secondly, in our entire constitutional history, I know of no example where Congress has enacted a law to expand or extend a war, over the explicit objection of the President. And this should not be the first such occasion. So, should we end the war? Yes.

Second, could you eventually, when the facts on the ground allow, repeal the AUMF without leaving legal gaps in our authority to target or detain? And the answer is, "yes," when the situation on the ground permits.

With regard to both targeting and detention, think of it as belt and suspenders. Last May, the President signed a Presidential policy guidance that formalized the executive branch's targeting practice and made clear that they conform to domestic and international law. And that lawfulness of this executive branch action depends on two things: the existence of an armed conflict with al-Qaeda, the Taliban, and associated forces, but it separately—and this is the suspenders part—rests on the President's lawful authority to act in self-defense against continuing and imminent threats to the United States.

Now, if al-Qaeda is defeated on the ground and you do not need to have an armed conflict with them, but all threats are not ended, you can remove the belt—namely, repeal the AUMF—and still have enough legal authority on your side through the Law of Self-Defense. And I describe, on pages 7 to 9 of my testimony, that if Congress would like this to be done in a statute, as opposed to Article 2 constitutional authority, it could codify the self-defense authority with regard to continuing and imminent threats so that the Congress could place conditions on reporting and the like.

What about detention? Same thing. If the facts on the ground lead to the situation where the United States has transitioned Afghan detention to Afghan control, where traditional detention tools can be used for some of the other individuals and can work with Congress on a plan to close Guantanamo, at that point there would be no need for Law of War detention authority. What the AUMF gives you is the authority to act against belligerent combatants as targets or as detainees. And if you do not need to do that anymore, you do not need the AUMF anymore.

Third, and finally, does it make sense to amend the AUMF? My view is, to expand it and create an ongoing war is not a good idea. No new legislation is better than bad new legislation. But, if Congress wants to set the stage for repeal by narrowing the AUMF, I suggest, in pages 12 through 14 of my written statement, how this could be done, and I suggest four particular steps Congress might consider: first, a sunset provision; second, stronger congressional reporting requirements; third, stronger public reporting requirements, particularly about civilian casualties; and finally, exploration of some kind of post/ex-post external review mechanism to examine the legality of past drone strikes.

So, in closing, the three goals—eventually ending the war, eventually seeking repeal, and narrowing the AUMF—are important, they are achievable, and they are worthy of thoughtful consideration by this committee and Congress.

My point is simple. The AUMF is not the only law we have. We have other laws. We should not treat the AUMF as a perpetual all-purpose security blanket that can be distorted and that will itself become a distorting force.

We can, in time, when the facts on the ground permit, repeal the AUMF and rely on other authorities to fill these gaps. And not to do so, from that point, I think would be bad for our counterterrorism policy and bad for our Constitution.

Thank you.

[The prepared statement of Mr. Koh follows:]

PREPARED STATEMENT OF HAROLD KONGJU KOH

Thank you, Mr. Chairman and Members of the committee, for inviting me before this committee today.

I am Sterling Professor of International Law at the Yale Law School, where since 1985, I have taught international law, national security law, and the law of U.S. foreign relations.[1] For 10 years, I served in the U.S. Government, most recently from 2009 to 2013 as Legal Adviser of the U.S. Department of State.[2] Having worked daily during my time as Legal Adviser on counterterrorism issues, I appear today to support the President's commitment, stated in his important speech at the National Defense University last May, to "continue to fight terrorism without keeping America on a perpetual wartime footing."[3]

When President Obama took office, the United States was engaged in congressionally authorized armed conflicts in Iraq, Afghanistan, and against al-Qaeda and its co-belligerents. Since then, the Iraq conflict has ended.[4] The President has declared his intent to withdraw combat troops from Afghanistan by the end of this calendar year.[5]

Today, let me explain why, after Iraq and Afghanistan, this country's counterterrorism policy should include three important and achievable elements of the President's NDU proposal: ending the war with al-Qaeda and its co-belligerents; repealing the Authorization for Use of Military Force (AUMF) enacted on September 18, 2001;[6] and prior to repeal, narrowing the AUMF's mandate. I agree with the President: first, that the armed conflict that began against al-Qaeda and its co-belligerents nearly 13 years ago, "like all wars, must end"; second, that Congress should aim to "ultimately repeal, the mandate" of the AUMF; and third, that in the interim, Congress should explore ways to narrow the AUMF rather than "to expand the AUMF's mandate further."[7]

I. ENDING THE WAR WITH AL-QAEDA AND ITS COBELLIGERENTS

In 4 months time, this coming September, the United States armed conflict with al-Qaeda will turn 13 years old. That is 9 years longer than either the Civil War or World War II, and nearly 5 years longer than the Revolutionary War. As I argued last year in a speech at Oxford, this conflict has become so protracted that it has come to feel like a "Forever War."[8] It has changed the nature of our foreign policy, consumed our new Millennium, and made it hard to remember what the world looked like before September 11.

In his NDU speech last May, the President summarized why we should reject indefinite war in favor of an "exit strategy" to bring this protracted conflict with al-Qaeda, like all wars, to an end:

> [T]he choices we make about war can impact—in sometimes unintended ways—the openness and freedom on which our way of life depends. *And that is why I intend to engage Congress about the existing Authorization to Use Military Force, or AUMF, to determine how we can continue to fight terrorism without keeping America on a perpetual wartime footing* . . . The Afghan war is coming to an end. Core al-Qaeda is a shell of its former self. Groups like AQAP must be dealt with, but in the years to come, not every collection of thugs that label themselves al-Qaeda will pose a credible threat to the United States. Unless we discipline our thinking, our definitions, our actions, we may be drawn into more wars we don't need to fight, or continue to grant Presidents unbound powers more suited for traditional armed conflicts between nation states.[9]

Last October, I argued that despite public skepticism, without fanfare, President Obama has made slow but steady progress toward achieving three key elements of his effort to end the Forever War: (1) disengaging from Afghanistan; (2) closing Guantanamo; and (3) disciplining drones.[10] The government witnesses you heard from earlier today have clarified how efforts in all three of those arenas continue.[11]

As outlined in the President's NDU speech, the administration's counterterrorism strategy treats "kill and capture" as only a small part of a much broader U.S. "smart power" strategy toward counterterrorism.[12] Within that broader strategy, the President insists upon maintaining a lawful and workable framework to govern our use of force against al-Qaeda and its associated forces, now formalized in Presidential Policy Guidance that President Obama signed last May. "In the Afghan war theater," the President said, "we must—and will—continue to support our troops until the transition is complete at the end of 2014 [by continuing] to take strikes against high value al-Qaeda targets, but also against forces that are massing to support attacks on coalition forces."[13] But "[b]eyond the Afghan theater," the President clarified, "we only target al-Qaeda and its associated forces. And even then, the use of drones is heavily constrained" by four principles, which are clearly enumerated in the important Fact Sheet that accompanied the President's NDU speech:[14] (1) the priority of capture over kill;[15] (2) respect for international law and state sovereignty;[16] (3) the requirement that targets present a "continuing and imminent threat" to U.S. persons[17] and (4) a "near-certainty" test for avoiding civilian casualties. At the same time, the President remains committed to maintaining a clear, lawful, and workable framework to govern detention of al-Qaeda and its associated forces at Guantanamo and elsewhere.[18] Finally, the President committed himself to transparency and consultation with Congress and our allies,[19] and to considering future workable proposals to extend oversight of lethal actions outside of active warzones.[20] Each of these key principles—a smart-power strategy, legal frameworks to govern drones and detention, and a commitment to transparency, consultation, and oversight—seems to me both correct and worth supporting.

For our country, peace is the norm and war is the exception. Condoning a state of perpetual war would mark a gross deviation from our constitutional norms. We need not, and should not, allow a wartime footing to become a perpetual state of affairs. Applying the President's declared principles steadily over time, we can end the war against al-Qaeda and its allies when circumstances on the ground allow, and while so doing, continue to meet all our domestic and international law obligations.

43

The President's speech more than a year ago made clear his intent to work with Members of Congress to "refine and ultimately repeal" the 2001 AUMF. He expressly stated, "I will not sign laws designed to expand this mandate further." [21] Nevertheless, some argue that the AUMF must continue, or even be expanded, despite the President's clearly stated position. They claim that repealing the 2001 AUMF will leave legal "gaps" [22] in both the President's targeting and detention authority that will prevent the Executive from successfully protecting America and our allies from known as well as future terrorist threats.

As a policy matter, any proposal to expand and extend the AUMF's mandate would be both unprecedented and exceedingly unwise. After more than three decades of studying, writing, and teaching the law of U.S. foreign policy, I know of no example in our long constitutional history where the Congress—traditionally the branch that seeks to end wars—has enacted a law expressly to extend or expand a war over the President's explicit objection. [23]

As a legal matter, the President's goal of "refining, then repealing" the AUMF is both achievable and sustainable without undermining the security of the American people. Substantial legal authorities for both targeting and incapacitation of terrorists were available to the Executive branch before the 2001 AUMF. These authorities have been significantly strengthened since then, and would remain in its absence. [24] The current legal authorities are sufficient to provide the administration with all the authority needed to address threats to the United States. At the proper time, the President and Congress can work together to repeal the 2001 AUMF without risking exposing our population to future threats.

A. Targeting

As I argued as Legal Adviser and continue to believe, the Executive branch is employing lawful standards for targeting both: (1) Taliban and al-Qaeda combatants in Afghanistan, and (2) al-Qaeda, the Taliban, and "associated forces" both inside and outside of Afghanistan. [25] As the administration has explained, the U.S. Government defines "associated forces" in accordance with international law to include those (1) organized armed groups that have entered the fight alongside al-Qaeda; and (2) are a co-belligerent with al-Qaeda in the hostilities against the United States and its coalition partners. [26] While not part of the 2001 AUMF's wording, the term "associated forces" derived from a shared Executive [27] and judicial interpretation of the statute's text [28] used to clarify the authority of the AUMF in aftermath of 9/11, which was later codified in the 2012 NDAA. [29] As now construed by all three branches of government, the 2001 AUMF authorizes all necessary and appropriate force against al-Qaeda, the Taliban, and associated forces under U.S. law. Those strikes are lawful under international law because the Obama administration's standards—as expressed in the President's May 2013 NDU speech and accompanying Presidential Policy Guidance—construe the AUMF to be read consistently with international humanitarian law, which our Supreme Court has held governs the Non-International Armed Conflict (NIAC) in which the United States is currently engaged against al-Qaeda and associated forces. [30]

That said, the 2001 AUMF is not needed as a perpetual legal authority. It can be repealed at the appropriate time, once al-Qaeda has been effectively defeated. At that time, repeal would create no "legal gap" if the United States found an ongoing need to strike particular remaining al-Qaeda terrorists and associated forces who pose a continuing and imminent threat to the United States. In such cases, future strikes against groups that pose a continuing and imminent threat to the United States could still be justified under both domestic and international law.

As a constitutional matter, it has long been settled that "[a]s Commander in Chief and Chief Executive, [the President] may use the Armed Forces to protect the Nation and its people." [31] In the Prize Cases, the Supreme Court affirmed the President's inherent authority to use force in self-defense to protect the Nation against invasion or sudden attack, declaring that "[i]f a war be made by invasion of a foreign nation, the President is not only authorized but bound to resist force by force. He does not initiate the war, but is bound to accept the challenge without waiting for any special legislative authority." [32] Under the principle of self-defense that is inherent in the President's Commander in Chief authority, the President has long been understood to have constitutional authority to act reasonably in self-defense against any threat. [33]

Read in light of international law, that constitutional authority would clearly include the right to act against "imminent" threats, a term defined in the famous *Caroline* case as applying to situations in which the "necessity of that self-defence is instant, overwhelming, and leaving no choice of means, and no moment for deliberation.''[34] But under a very narrow set of circumstances, the *Caroline* requirement may also reasonably be read to permit direct strikes as a last resort against groups or individuals who pose a continuing and imminent threat [35] by virtue of: (1) engaging in ''a concerted pattern of continuing armed activity'' [36] directed against the U.S.—i.e., demonstrating a willingness to attack the U.S. if given the opportunity; (2) past successful attacks; and (3) ''actively planning, threatening, or perpetrating [future] armed attacks'' [37] against America.[38] In my judgment, this understanding of imminence is consistent with Article 51 of the U.N. Charter, which codifies the right of national and collective self-defense.[39]

President Obama essentially embraced this concept in his 2013 NDU speech when he said-regarding the use of force outside the Afghan theater—''America does not take strikes to punish individuals; we act against terrorists who pose a continuing and imminent threat to the American people, and when there are no other governments capable of effectively addressing the threat.[40] If, after the Afghan conflict ends, the Executive wishes to continue conducting strikes in Afghanistan against local groups or individuals that do not pose a continuing and imminent threat to the U.S., the President would need to seek separate legal authority from Congress. But as President Obama noted in his NDU speech, the ''future of terrorism'' is ''lethal yet less capable al-Qaeda affiliates; threats to diplomatic facilities and businesses abroad; homegrown extremists,'' [41] a threat that would require a range of tools.[42] With respect to both continuing and imminent terrorist threats and new threats that meet the relevant constitutional and international law tests, these tools should give the President sufficient legal authority to conduct the activities necessary to protect the American population.

I fully understand why Congress might prefer not to leave a matter of such importance to inherent constitutional authority. If so, Congress could both clarify and narrow the scope of the AUMF going forward by codifying a standard authorizing the principles stated in the President's May 2013 Presidential Policy Guidance. Such a standard, consistent with the international law arguments outlined above, would authorize the President to use force against those groups or individuals who pose a continuing and imminent threat to the U.S. by virtue of: (1) having already attacked the U.S.; (2) engaging in a concerted pattern of continuing armed activity directed against the U.S.; and (3) actively planning, threatening, or perpetrating armed attacks against the U.S. Congressional action to codify the authority that the President needs to effectively confront post-9/11 threats would update the language of the AUMF to reflect the administration's actual policies, now embodied in executive branch mandates. Such a reading would draw what the President called an important ''distinction between the capacity and reach of a bin Laden and a network that is actively planning major terrorist plots against the homeland versus jihadists who are engaged in various local power struggles and disputes, often sectarian.'' [43]

If government officials are too loose in who they consider to be forces ''associated with'' al-Qaeda, then we will always have new enemies, and the Forever War will continue forever.[44] Instead of continuing to rely on the broadly worded 2001 AUMF to codify a permanent state of war, it would be far better to narrow the scope of targeting authority to match current policy. This would both give Congress greater say in authorizing force and bolster the constitutional legitimacy of counterterrorism operations by giving the President's current standards a shared legislative and executive imprimatur.[45]

B. Detention

Nor should repealing the AUMF create any ''legal gap'' in detaining and trying future terrorist detainees in either American courts or elsewhere.[46] As President Obama reiterated in both his 2013 NDU speech and his 2014 State of the Union Address,[47] his administration is committed to transferring the Parwan detention facility to Afghan control, closing Guantanamo, transferring the prisoners held there to other countries, trying them in Article III courts in the United States, or trying them before military commissions.

As for Parwan, the United States has already transitioned detention operations to Afghan authorities.[48] The end of major combat operations in Afghanistan may well also lead to renewed legal challenges to the President's authority to continue to detain at least some of the detainees at Guantanamo.[49] But as the testimonies of Mr. Preston and Ms. McLeod make clear, executive branch lawyers are carefully studying this possibility, and assessing the effect it might have on law of war detention under the 2012 NDAA.

While some have expressed concern over so-called ''unreleasable'' prisoners still at Guantanamo, as the executive branch report submitted last week under the terms of the National Defense Authorization Act makes clear, that problem can be managed in a number of ways.[50] This ''legacy issue'' should not become ''the tail wagging not only the debate over closing Guantanamo, but the debate over repealing/replacing the AUMF.''[51] Once Congress and the President come to an agreement on how to handle the prisoners currently being held at Guantanamo, repealing the AUMF should leave no gap in America's detention authority.[52]

In any event, we should not confuse the past with the future. The President has repeatedly declared his intent to close Guantanamo and not to bring any new detainees there. Thus, debates over continuing authority to hold those currently in law of war detention—a population that the President has expressly declared his intent to minimize or eliminate—lend little support to the claim that new legal authority is somehow needed to ensure potential future detentions of dangerous terrorist suspects. The administration has now developed an effective scheme for detaining and trying defendants in Article III courts, which it recently executed effectively against Sulaiman Abu Ghaith, the most senior bin Laden associate to be tried and convicted in a civilian court in the United States since 9/11, and the radical cleric Abu Hamza al-Masri, who was convicted by a federal court this week on 11 criminal counts.[53] Two other Article III defendants, Ahmed Warsame (who pleaded guilty) and Abu Anas al Libi (who is currently awaiting trial), were initially detained for a period of questioning under AUMF authority, before being given Miranda warnings and charged criminally under sealed indictments.[54] Under laws passed since 9/11, the government should have ample authority, even without the AUMF, to pick up future terrorism suspects overseas.[55]

III. NARROWING THE AUMF

While eventual repeal of the 2001 AUMF remains the best long-term way to finally bring an end to the Forever War, the precise timing of that repeal remains a decision about which the administration and Congress should agree, based upon the facts as they develop. Some, however, have invited Congress to consider proposals broadly to ''update'' the AUMF to address new threats.[56] To the extent that those proposals amount to proposals to expand, extend, or perpetuate the war with al-Qaeda and its co-belligerents—and to extend it to currently unknown, future terrorist organizations—I believe they are both unwise and unnecessary. In the interim, no legislation would be plainly better than new legislation for its own sake.

Others claim that Congress could prepare the way for eventual repeal of the AUMF by refining and narrowing—but not expanding—the scope of the 2001 AUMF. Their claim is that reform to narrow the AUMF could, first, resolve uncertainties about the continued legality and currency of a counterterrorism framework that remains tied to 9/11, an event that transpired 13 years ago; second, bring the text of the AUMF more into line with the landscape of post-9/11 threats; and third, provide Congress with an opportunity to reassert its role in defining and limiting the authorities of the executive branch. While I do not see pre-repeal reform as either wise or necessary, if Congress wishes to consider reforms to refine and narrow (and not expand) the AUMF's broad authorization, it would make the most sense to include within the AUMF a sunset clause, which would provide increased opportunities for congressional and Executive dialogue and force debate and voting at timed intervals. As Representative Adam Schiff noted when proposing stand-alone legislation that would sunset the 2001 AUMF beginning in 2015, concurrent with the end of combat operations in Afghanistan, ''When Congress passed the AUMF shortly after 9/11, we did not intend to authorize a war without end.''[57] Because the current war against nonstate actors responsible for 9/11 will not have a conventional end marked by a peace treaty, Congress could amend the 2001 AUMF, without narrowing its substantive scope, by adding a sunset provision—of one year, or perhaps timed to coincide with the Afghan drawdown—to ensure that both elected branches play a role in deciding whether and when the U.S. will use force against al-Qaeda and associated forces going forward. Adding a sunset clause would also help to ensure that the statutory framework for our counterterrorism operations is regularly updated to reflect the realities of the threats we are facing, and to accurately express the intent and will of the legislative branch.[58]

To improve public and congressional access to information, Congress could further amend the AUMF by codifying more stringent transparency and reporting requirements. Strengthened congressional reporting requirements might require that relevant committees regularly receive information on secret military and covert operations, including requiring that Congress be informed as to which groups are covered under the AUMF and in which nations the Department of Defense believes Congress has authorized the President to use military force.[59]

These confidential reporting provisions could be strengthened by adding public reporting requirements, which might include requiring the periodic public release of nonsensitive information as to where and against whom the President is using military force under congressional authorization. Such reports are regularly given in the context of the War Powers Resolution, and it should not unduly burden the Executive to require that similar information also be given here.[60] Nor do I see why the President should not be asked to issue a regular public report on the number of combatants and civilians killed by the United States use of targeted lethal force abroad. Unfortunately, a similar provision was recently stripped out of congressional legislation, which would have required President Obama to make public each year the number of people killed or injured in targeted killing operations.[61] Such transparency would help rebut a wave of drone reports—by Human Rights Watch and Amnesty International, and the United Nations Special Rapporteur on Counterterrorism and Human Rights and Extrajudicial Killings—that have challenged whether the strict standards stated in the President's NDU speech have in fact been consistently and rigorously applied.[62] These NGO reports do not assess the total number or rate of civilian casualties for all U.S. drone strikes.[63] Nor do they say that all U.S. targeted killings are illegal. They do, however, claim that dozens of civilians have been killed, and that the U.S. may be misinterpreting and misapplying existing law by applying broader notions of targetability and imminence than international law permits. These are serious charges that deserve serious responses from our government, which is why I argued a year ago, and continue to believe, that the administration

> Should make public its full legal explanation for why and when it is consistent with due process of law to target American citizens and residents. . . . [I]t should clarify its method of counting civilian casualties, and what that method is consistent with international humanitarian law standards. [And] where factual disputes exist about the threat level against which past drone strikes were directed, the administration should release the factual record. By so doing, it could explain what gave it cause to believe that particular threats were imminent, what called for the immediate exercise of self-defense, and what demonstrated either the express consent of the territorial sovereign or the inability and unwillingness of those sovereigns to suppress a legitimate threat.[64]

Finally, exploration and eventual implementation of some form of ex post review mechanism for targeting would be beneficial both as a policy and a legal matter.[65] The President's own guidelines already state that targeting policies should be reviewed for legality.[66] In his NDU speech, the President asked his lawyers to consider a special court or an Executive review board as possible ways to extend oversight of lethal actions outside of the Afghan theater.[67] Because European courts are showing increased initiative in reviewing European cooperation in targeting operations for compliance with domestic and international law,[68] some form of ex post judicial review of these actions may prove inevitable in the near future, whether American officials favor it or not.

In sum, while I do not favor legislation for its own sake, until the AUMF is ultimately repealed, Congress need not be a passive rubber-stamp. If Congress wants to play a proactive role in resolving legal uncertainties, it could tighten the language of the current AUMF to narrow substantive scope and improve accountability. Amending the 2001 AUMF to narrow and refine its authority could enhance the legitimacy of our counterterrorism operations in ways that would encourage information-sharing and multilateral cooperation going forward. As former FBI Director Robert S. Mueller III noted, ''Our enemies live in the seams of our jurisdictions. No single agency or nation can find them and fight them alone. If we are to protect our citizens, working together is not just the best option, it is the only option.'' [69] Short-term refinements to the scope of the AUMF in anticipation of its eventual repeal could send a positive signal to the international community of the United States commitment to complying with its domestic and international legal obligations and ending the Forever War.

IV. CONCLUSION

For the foregoing reasons, I believe that ending the war with al-Qaeda and its co-belligerents, eventually repealing the AUMF, and narrowing its mandate in the meantime are all important and achievable elements of this administration's counterterrorism policy.

Thank you for your attention. I now look forward to answering any questions the committee might have.

———————————

End Notes

[1] I am grateful to Hank Moon and Mara Revkin of the Yale Law School for their help in preparing this testimony. Although I sit on a law school faculty as well as on the boards of several organizations, the views expressed here are mine alone, not those of my colleagues or of any of the institutions with which I am affiliated.

[2] I previously served in the Clinton Administration as Assistant Secretary of State for Democracy, Human Rights and Labor from 1998–2001, and in the Reagan Administration as Attorney-Adviser at the Office of Legal Counsel of the U.S. Department of Justice from 1983–85.

[3] Remarks by the President at the National Defense University, White House Office of the Press Secretary (May 23, 2013) [hereinafter Obama NDU Speech].

[4] See Authorization for Use of Military Force Against Iraq Resolution of 2002, Pub. L. No. 107–243, 116 Stat. 1498. On August 31, 2010, President Obama declared an end to the combat mission in Iraq. See Helene Cooper & Sheryl Gay Stolberg, "Obama Declares an End to Combat Mission in Iraq," N.Y. Times, Aug. 31, 2010.

[5] On December 1, 2009, President Obama announced his intent to withdraw troops from Afghanistan. See The White House Office of the Press Sec'y, Remarks by the President in Address to the Nation on the Way Forward in Afghanistan and Pakistan (December 1, 2009). The number of U.S. troops remaining in Afghanistan after the planned drawdown could drop below the originally projected figure of 10,000, reflecting "a belief among White House officials that Afghan security forces have evolved into a robust enough force to contain a still-potent Taliban-led insurgency." Missy Ryan & Arshad Mohammed, "U.S. Force in Afghanistan May be Cut to Less Than 10,000 Troops," Reuters, Apr. 21, 2014.

[6] See Authorization for Use of Military Force, Pub. L. No. 107–40, 115 Stat. 224, 224 (2001) (codified at 50 U.S.C. 1541 note) [hereinafter 2001 AUMF] ("That the President is authorized to use all necessary and appropriate force against those nations, organizations, or persons he determines planned, authorized, committed, or aided the terrorist attacks that occurred on September 11, 2001, or harbored such organizations or persons in order to prevent any future acts of international terrorism against the United States by such nations, organizations. or persons.").

[7] Obama NDU Speech, supra note 3.

[8] See Harold Hongju Koh, "How to End the Forever War," Speech at Oxford Union (May 7, 2013) [Koh Oxford Speech].

[9] See Obama NDU Speech, supra note 3 (emphasis added).

[10] See Harold Hongju Koh, "Ending the Forever War: A Progress Report," Just Security (Oct. 28, 2013, 3:00 PM) [hereinafter Koh Progress Report].

[11] See testimonies of Department of Defense General Counsel Stephen Preston and Principal Deputy Legal Adviser Mary McLeod before the Senate Foreign Relations Committee on May 21, 2014.

[12] See Obama NDU Speech, supra note 3 ("[T]he use of force must be seen as part of a larger discussion we need to have about a comprehensive counterterrorism strategy—because for all the focus on the use of force, force alone cannot make us safe. We cannot use force everywhere that a radical ideology takes root; and in the absence of a strategy that reduces the wellspring of extremism, a perpetual war—through drones or Special Forces or troop deployments—will prove self-defeating, and alter our country in troubling ways. . . . [T]he next element of our strategy involves addressing the underlying grievances and conflicts that feed extremism—from North Africa to South Asia.").

[13] Id.

[14] See U.S. Policy Standards and Procedures for the Use of Force in Counterterrorism Operations Outside the United States and Areas of Active Hostilities, White House (May 23, 2013) [hereinafter Summary of White House PPG] ("Lethal force will be used only to prevent or stop attacks against U.S. persons, and even then, only when capture is not feasible and no other reasonable alternatives exist to address the threat effectively. In particular, lethal force will be used outside areas of active hostilities only when the following preconditions are met:

First, there must be a legal basis for using lethal force, whether it is against a senior operational leader of a terrorist organization or the forces that organization is using or intends to use to conduct terrorist attacks.

Second, the United States will use lethal force only against a target that poses a continuing, imminent threat to U.S. persons. It is simply not the case that all terrorists pose a continuing, imminent threat to U.S. persons; if a terrorist does not pose such a threat, the United States will not use lethal force.

Third, the following criteria must be met before lethal action may be taken:

1. Near certainty that the terrorist target is present;

2. Near certainty that noncombatants will not be injured or killed.") [The appended footnote further clarifies that "Noncombatants are individuals who may not be made the object of attack under applicable international law. The term 'noncombatant' does not include an individual who is part of a belligerent party to an armed conflict, an individual who is taking a direct part in hostilities, or an individual who is targetable in the exercise of national self-defense. Males of military age may be noncombatants; it is not the case that all military-aged males in the vicinity of a target are deemed to be combatants."]

3. An assessment that capture is not feasible at the time of the operation;

4. An assessment that the relevant governmental authorities in the country where action is contemplated cannot or will not effectively address the threat to U.S. persons; and

5. An assessment that no other reasonable alternatives exist to effectively address the threat to U.S. persons. Finally, whenever the United States uses force in foreign territories, international legal principles, including respect for sovereignty and the law of armed conflict, impose important constraints on the ability of the United

States to act unilaterally—and on the way in which the United States can use force. The United States respects national sovereignty and international law.

[15] Id. ("America does not take strikes when we have the ability to capture individual terrorists; our preference is always to detain, interrogate, and prosecute. [A]s a matter of policy, the preference of the United States is to capture terrorist suspects.")

[16] Id. ("America cannot take strikes wherever we choose; our actions are bound by consultations with partners, and respect for state sovereignty.")

[17] Id. ("America does not take strikes to punish individuals; we act against terrorists who pose a continuing and imminent threat to the American people, and when there are no other governments capable of effectively addressing the threat.")

[18] Id. ("Today, I once again call on Congress to lift the restrictions on detainee transfers from GTMO.")

[19] Id. ("I've insisted on strong oversight of all lethal action. After I took office, my administration began briefing all strikes outside of Iraq and Afghanistan to the appropriate committees of Congress. . . . [I] do not believe it would be constitutional for the government to target and kill any U.S. citizen—with a drone, or with a shotgun—without due process, nor should any President deploy armed drones over U.S. soil.")

[20] Id. ("Going forward, I've asked my administration to review proposals to extend oversight of lethal actions outside of warzones that go beyond our reporting to Congress.")

[21] See Obama NDU Speech, supra note 3.

[22] See, e.g., Robert Chesney, Jack Goldsmith, Matthew C. Waxman & Benjamin Wittes, "A Statutory Framework for Next-Generation Terrorist Threats," Hoover Inst. at Stanford Univ. 6 (2013) [hereinafter Hoover Report] (Authors are "skeptical" that the President's inherent powers under Article II combined with ordinary law enforcement tools "[a]re adequate to address any gap that may emerge between what defense of the nation demands and what law enforcement and intelligence options can provide in extra-AUMF scenarios.").

[23] See, e.g., Melvin Small, "Democracy and Diplomacy: The Impact of Domestic Politics in U.S. Foreign Policy," 1789–1994, 30 (1996) (a congressional declaration of war without Presidential approval "has never happened . . ."); Jennifer K. Elsea & Richard F. Grimmett, "Declarations of War and Authorizations for the Use of Military Force: Historical Background and Legal Implications 1" (2007) (when Congress has legislated authorizations for the use of force rather than formal declarations of war, "[i]n most cases, the President has requested the authority, but Congress has sometimes given the President less than what he asked for."). Theoretically, Congress may by a two-thirds majority declare war over the objections of the President, but "[i]n practice, such a situation cannot be imagined." Stephen Vladeck, "Why a Drone Court Won't Work—But (Nominal) Damages Might," Lawfare (Feb. 10, 2013, 5:12 PM) [Vladeck Drone Court].

[24] These include various statutory authorities and other agencies to make arrests, which are not territorially limited (e.g., 18 U.S.C. 3052), as well as extraterritorial expansions in civilian criminal statutes especially 18 U.S.C. 2339B. For a review of the various legal changes that have led to a dramatic increase in counterterrorism capacities since 2001, see generally Jennifer C. Daskal & Stephen I. Vladeck, "After the AUMF," Harv. Natl. Secur. J. 115, 132–37 (2014) [hereinafter Daskal & Vladeck, After the AUMF].

[25] See Harold Hongju Koh, Legal Adviser, U.S. Dept. of State, "The Obama Administration and International Law," Address to the American Society of International Law (Mar. 25, 2010) [hereinafter Koh Speech] (noting that all operations by the U.S. Government must comply with international humanitarian law).

[26] See, e.g., Jeh Charles Johnson, General Counsel, U.S. Dep't of Def., "The Conflict Against Al Qaeda and its Affiliates: How Will It End?" Speech Before the Oxford Union (Nov. 30, 2012) [hereinafter Johnson Oxford Speech].

[27] The term "associated forces" first appeared in a Department of Justice habeas brief filed during the early days of the Obama administration, on March 13, 2009, which argued that the President has authority to detain those who "substantially support" Al Qaeda or the Taliban and "associated forces." Marty Lederman & Steve Vladeck, "The NDAA: The Good, the Bad, and the Laws of War—Part II," Lawfare Blog (Dec. 31, 2011, 4:48 PM). The then-new Obama administration offered this narrowed executive interpretation of the AUMF in response to calls from many, including myself, to clarify and narrow the Executive's tendency to "construe the vaguely worded Authorization for Use of Military Force (AUMF) Resolution to override existing legislation . . ." See Statement of Harold Hongju Koh Before the Senate Judiciary Committee, Subcommittee on The Constitution on Restoring the Rule of Law, Sept. 16, 2008.

[28] In Hamlily v. Obama, 616 F. Supp. 2d 63, 78 (D.D.C. 2009), Judge Bates of the U.S. District Court for the District of Columbia accepted the Obama administration's interpretation of the AUMF, holding that "[t]he President also has the authority to detain persons who are or were part of Taliban or al-Qaeda forces or associated forces that are engaged in hostilities against the United States." The D.C. Circuit has since adopted this language on multiple occasions. See, e.g., Al-Bihani v. Obama, 590 F.3d 866, 872 (D.C. Cir. 2010); Barhoumi v. Obama, 609 F.3d 416, 432 (D.C. Cir. 2010).

[29] See FY 2012 NDAA § 1021(b)(2), 125 Stat. at 1562 [hereinafter 2012 NDAA] (authorizing detention of "[a] person who was a part of or substantially supported al-Qaeda, the Taliban, or associated forces that are engaged in hostilities against the United States or its coalition partners, including any person who has committed a belligerent act or has directly supported such hostilities in aid of such enemy forces"). See also Hussain v. Obama, 718 F.3d 964, 967 (D.C. Cir. 2013) (citing the 2012 NDAA to hold that the AUMF authorizes the President to detain individuals who are part of Al Qaeda, the Taliban, or "associated forces"). I should caution that no court has yet considered whether precisely the same legal standards for membership in or co-belligerency with al-Qaeda should apply to determine whether an individual is targetable, as opposed to detainable. To trigger a legal right of self-defense sufficient to target an individual,

the United States might well be required to demonstrate that the individual has played a senior operational role capable of generating a continuing and imminent threat to the United States.

[30] See generally Koh Speech, supra note 25 (discussing relevant international law standards). In *Hamdan* v. *Rumsfeld*, 548 U.S. 557 (2006), the Supreme Court held that the U.S. was engaged in a NIAC with al-Qaeda, and was therefore bound by Common Article 3, a provision appearing in all four Geneva Conventions, "which provides that, in a conflict not of an international character occurring in the territory of one of the High Contracting Parties [i.e., signatories], each Party to the conflict shall be bound to apply, as a minimum, certain provisions protecting [p]ersons . . . placed hors de combat by . . . detention, including a prohibition on the passing of sentences . . . without previous judgment . . . by a regularly constituted court affording all the judicial guarantees . . . recognized as indispensable by civilized peoples." Id. at 562 (quotations omitted).

[31] See *United States* v. *Verdugo-Urquidez*, 494 U.S. 259 (1990).

[32] See The Prize Cases, 67 U.S. (2 Black) 635, 668 (1863).

[33] See Daskal & Vladeck, "After the AUMF," supra note 24 ("[I]t is well settled that the President has inherent authority under Article II of the U.S. Constitution and Article 51 of the U.N. Charter to take immediate—and, where necessary, lethal—action in defense of the nation," while noting that the authority to engage in self-defense under Article II is not unlimited).

[34] Department of State, Letter from Mr. Webster to Lord Ashburton, Washington, Aug. 6, 1842.

[35] See Daniel Bethlehem, "Self-Defense Against an Imminent or Actual Armed Attack by Nonstate Actors," 106 Am. J. Int'l L. 769 (2012) [hereinafter Bethlehem Self-Defense Principles].

[36] As former Legal Adviser to the Foreign and Commonwealth Office of the United Kingdom, Sir Daniel Bethlehem, explained: "While 'imminence' continues to be a key element of the law relevant to anticipatory self-defense in response to a threat of attack, the concept needs to be further refined and developed to take into account the new circumstances and threats from nonstate actors that states face today." Id. at 5.

[37] Id. at 6 ("Armed action in self-defense may be directed against those actively planning, threatening, or perpetrating armed attacks. It may also be directed against those in respect of whom there is a strong, reasonable, and objective basis for concluding that they are taking a direct part in those attacks through the provision of material support essential to the attacks.").

[38] As one commentator recently put it, "There is . . . support for the argument that a state facing an impending devastating attack cannot be expected to have to wait for it to actually strike its cities before engaging in forcible self-defence." See Noam Lubell, "The Problem of Imminence in an Uncertain World 5" (M. Weller, ed., "The Oxford Handbook of the Use of Force in International Law," forthcoming 2014) ("There does appear to be a growing number of views that support preemptive action when limited to imminent attacks," particularly against those terrorist networks that have previously attacked a country successfully.").

[39] U.N. Charter art. 51 ("Nothing in the present Charter shall impair the inherent right of individual or collective self-defence if an armed attack occurs against a Member of the United Nations, until the Security Council has taken measures necessary to maintain international peace and security."). By so saying, let me make clear that I am not supporting the considerably broader notion of "preemptive self-defense" favored by some international lawyers, which I have long rejected. See, e.g., Harold Hongju Koh, "On American Exceptionalism," 55 Stanford L. Rev. 1479, 1516 ("Preemptive self-defense arguments cannot clearly distinguish between permitted defensive measures and forbidden assaults"); Harold Hongju Koh, Comment to Michael W. Doyle, "Striking First: Preemption and Prevention in International Conflict 99" (2011) (S. Macedo, ed.).

[40] See Obama NDU Speech, supra note 3. In 2012, CIA Director John Brennan, then-Assistant to the President for Homeland Security and Counterterrorism, similarly stated: "[T]he use of force against members of al-Qaeda is authorized under both international and U.S. law, including both the inherent right of national self-defense and the 2001 Authorization for Use of Military Force." John O. Brennan, Assistant to the President for Homeland Security and Counterterrorism, Speech at the Woodrow Wilson International Center for Scholars (Apr. 30, 2012).

[41] Id.

[42] See supra note 24.

[43] See David Remnick, "Going the Distance: On and Off the Road with Barack Obama," The New Yorker, Jan. 27, 2014 ("'The analogy we use around here sometimes, and I think is accurate, is if a jayvee team puts on Lakers uniforms that doesn't make them Kobe Bryant,' Obama said.").

[44] In recent War Powers Reports to Congress, for example, the administration has correctly taken pains to specify that "[t]he U.S. military has taken direct action in Somalia against members of al-Qaeda, including those who are also members of al-Shabaab, who are engaged in efforts to carry out terrorist attacks against the United States and our interests." Letter from President Barack Obama to Speaker of the House, Presidential Letter—2012 War Powers Resolution 6-Month Report (Jun. 15, 2012) [hereinafter 2012 War Powers Resolution 6-Month Report], ("the U.S. military has worked to counter the terrorist threat posed by al-Qaeda *and al-Qaeda-associated elements of al-Shabaab*") (emphasis added). By so saying, the administration has made clear that it has acted against particular individuals because they themselves are part of or co-belligerents with al-Qaeda, not because we are at war with all of al-Shabaab.

[45] Cf. Youngstown *Sheet & Tube Co.* v. *Sawyer*, 343 at 635–36 (Jackson, J., concurring) ("When the President acts pursuant to an express or implied authorization of Congress, his authority is at its maximum, for it includes all that he possesses in his own right plus all that Congress can delegate.").

[46] See generally *Daskal & Vladeck*, After the AUMF, supra note 24.

[47] Barack H. Obama, President of the United States, Remarks by the President in State of the Union Address (Jan. 28, 2014), ("with the Afghan war ending, this needs to be the year Congress lifts the remaining restrictions on detainee transfers and we close the prison at Guanta-

namo Bay—because we counter terrorism not just through intelligence and military action, but by remaining true to our constitutional ideals, and setting an example for the rest of the world.'').

[48] The March 9, 2012, Memorandum of Understanding (MOU) between Afghanistan and the United States transferred authority for Parwan detainees to Afghan control after a ''Transition period, which [was] not to last more than 6 months.'' Memorandum of Understanding between the Islamic Republic of Afghanistan and the United States of America on Transfer of U.S. Detention Facilities in Afghan Territory to Afghanistan (Mar. 9, 2012).

[49] See generally Marty Lederman,'' Justice Breyer's Intriguing Suggestions In Hussain: A Sign of Habeas Challenges to Come?'', Just Security (Apr. 23, 2014, 10:30 AM), (''[W]hen such active combat operations in Afghanistan do cease in the near future, and/or if and when the U.S. concludes that al-Qaeda's capabilities have been sufficiently degraded so that it is no longer a continuing threat to strike the U.S., attorneys for the GTMO detainees will begin to more strenuously press the argument that the continued detention of Taliban and al-Qaeda forces is no longer necessary and appropriate, on the theory that there will be no 'battle' to which the detainees might return''); Johnson Oxford Speech, supra note 26 (after al-Qaeda's defeat, ''[w]e will also need to face the question of what to do with any members of al-Qaeda who still remain in U.S. military detention without a criminal conviction and sentence. In general, the military's authority to detain ends with the ''cessation of active hostilities.'').

[50] See Charlie Savage, ''U.S. Report Addresses Concern Over Obama's Plan to Close Guantanamo,'' N.Y. Times, May 16, 2014, at A17. For the full text of the report, see U.S. Dep't of Justice, Report Pursuant to Section 1039 of the National Defense Authorization Act for Fiscal Year 2014 (May 14, 2014).

[51] Stephen I. Vladeck, ''Detention After the AUMF,'' 82 Fordham L. Rev. 2189 (2014).

[52] One recent proposal worth exploring may be ''[a] compromise solution wherein the government transfers or otherwise releases all of the detainees who have been cleared for transfer, moves all of the other detainees into the United States, and accepts a repeal of the AUMF in favor of a more specific authorization for long-term civil detention of those detainees who are too dangerous to be released, and yet who cannot be subjected to trial in civilian or military court.'' Stephen Vladeck, ''Detention After the AUMF,'' Just Security (Apr. 4, 2014, 1:39 PM). See also Benjamin Weiser, ''Jurors Convict Abu Ghaith, Bin Laden Son-in-Law, in Terror Case,'' N.Y. Times, Mar. 26, 2014. In light of reports that Yemen is making progress toward building a secure rehabilitation center to hold Guantanamo returnees, the increasing feasibility of transfers to Yemen and other third countries will reduce the number of detainees who would need to be held in long-term civil detention. See ''Yemen Takes Step to Set Up Secure Rehab for Guantanamo Detainees,'' Reuters, May 14, 2014.

[53] Abu Ghaith was convicted on three counts for which he could face life in prison. See Benjamin Weiser, ''Jurors Convict Abu Ghaith, Bin Laden Son-in-Law, in Terror Case,'' N.Y. Times, Mar. 26, 2014; Karen McVeigh, ''Abu Hamza Found Guilty of Terrorism Charges at New York Trial,'' The Guardian, May 19, 2014. (Statement of U.S. Attorney Preet Bharara) (''As we have seen in the Manhattan federal courthouse in trial after trial . . . these trials have been difficult, but they have been fair and open and prompt.'').

[54] After interrogation and charging, Warsame pleaded guilty in the Southern District of New York in 2011 and is awaiting sentencing. See Press Release, Federal Bureau of Investigations, Guilty Plea Unsealed in New York Involving Ahmed Warsame, a Senior Terrorist Leader and Liaison Between al-Shabaab and Al Qaeda in the Arabian Peninsula, for Providing Material Support to Both Terrorist Organizations (Mar. 25, 2013). See generally Charlie Savage, ''U.S. Tests New Approach to Terrorism Cases on Somali Suspect,'' N.Y. Times (Jul. 6, 2011). Abu Anas al Libi has pleaded not guilty to all charges, and currently awaits trial in the Southern District of New York. See Deborah Feyerick & Lateef Mungin, ''Alleged Al Qaeda Operative Abu Anal Al Libi Pleads Not Guilty,'' CNN (Oct. 15, 2013, 8:07 PM). See generally Koh Progress Report, supra note 10.

[55] These include the various statutory authorities enumerated in supra note 24. If Congress wished specifically to preserve the possibility of the kind of pre-presentment detention (used in the Warsame and Al-Libi cases) for the purpose of questioning surviving members of al-Qaeda or its co-belligerents about possible future attacks, it could narrow the AUMF's detention authority to cover just this narrow circumstance. Congress could also codify the preferences for counterterrorism operations already explicit in the Presidential Policy Guidance: (1) Capture over targeted killing; (2) Law enforcement over military action; and (3) Local government action in countries whose governments are able and willing. Summary of White House PPG, supra note 14. (''The policy of the United States is not to use lethal force when it is feasible to capture a terrorist suspect, because capturing a terrorist offers the best opportunity to gather meaningful intelligence and to mitigate and disrupt terrorist plots. Capture operations are conducted only against suspects who may lawfully be captured or otherwise taken into custody by the United States and only when the operation can be conducted in accordance with all applicable law and consistent with our obligations to other sovereign states.'').

[56] Compare Hoover Report, supra note 22, with Jennifer Daskal & Stephen Vladeck, ''After the AUMF, II: Daskal and Vladeck Reply,'' Lawfare (Mar. 18 2013, 7:16 PM), (noting that the Hoover proposal would entail ''a much more expansive use-of-force regime than that which currently exists.'').

[57] See Press Release: Rep. Adam Schiff to Introduce Legislation to Sunset Authorization for Use of Military Force (June. 10, 2013). See also H.R. 2324 Sunset to the Authorization for Use of Military Force Act (2013). In three different years, Rep. Barbara Lee (D-Calif.) and 33 cosponsors have also introduced a bill that would repeal the AUMF 180 days after passage. See H.R. 198, Repeal of the Authorization for Use of Military Force (2013), H.R.198 Bill Summary & Status, 113th Congress (2013-2014).

[58] The Patriot Act provides one model for sunset provisions, and illustrates how sunset clauses can force congressional debate at the time of reauthorization. See Uniting and Strengthening

America by Providing Appropriate Tools Required To Intercept and Obstruct Terrorism (USA PATRIOT) Act of 2001, Pub. L. No. 107–56, 115 Stat. 272.

[59] Such a provision would simply require as a matter of law what the President is already providing as a matter of policy. See Obama NDU Speech, supra note 3 ("After I took office, my administration began briefing all strikes outside of Iraq and Afghanistan to the appropriate committees of Congress. Let me repeat that: Not only did Congress authorize the use of force, it is briefed on every strike that America takes. Every strike. That includes the one instance when we targeted an American citizen—Anwar Awlaki, the chief of external operations for AQAP. This week, I authorized the declassification of this action, and the deaths of three other Americans in drone strikes, to facilitate transparency and debate on this issue and to dismiss some of the more outlandish claims that have been made.").

[60] For examples of recent war powers reports that include drone strikes, see 2012 War Powers Resolution 6-Month Report, supra note 44.

[61] See Mark Mazzetti, "Senate Drops Bid to Report on Drone Use," N.Y. Times, April 28, 2014.

[62] See Human Rights Watch, "Between a Drone and Al-Qaeda: The Civilian Cost of U.S. Targeted Killings in Yemen" (2013); Amnesty International, "Will I Be Next?: U.S. Drone Strikes in Pakistan" (2013); Philip Alston, "IHL, Transparency, and the Heyns' U.N. Drones Report," Just Security (Oct. 23, 2013, 4:15 PM).

[63] See Sarah Knuckey, "Human Rights Groups Release Investigation Reports into U.S. Targeted Killings: A Guide to the Issues," Just Security (Oct. 22, 2013, 12:02 AM).

[64] See Koh Oxford Speech, supra note 8.

[65] One commentator has noted that proposals for a "drone court" modeled after the Foreign Intelligence Surveillance Court (FISC) face "formidable legal and policy obstacles," but urges as a first step toward creating a meaningful regime of judicial supervision "the codification of a statutory cause of action for nominal damages . . . for those unlawfully injured by [drones] . . . ." Vladeck Drone Court, supra note 23.

[66] See Summary of White House PPG, supra note 14 ("Senior national security officials . . . and attorneys . . . including the senior lawyers of key departments and agencies—will review and determine the legality of proposals.").

[67] See Obama NDU Speech, supra note 3 ("The establishment of a special court to evaluate and authorize lethal action has the benefit of bringing a third branch of government into the process, but raises serious constitutional issues about Presidential and judicial authority. Another idea that's been suggested—the establishment of an independent oversight board in the executive branch—avoids those problems, but may introduce a layer of bureaucracy into national security decisionmaking, without inspiring additional public confidence in the process. But despite these challenges, I look forward to actively engaging Congress to explore these and other options for increased oversight.").

[68] British officials were recently the subject of a domestic civil lawsuit for allegedly sharing intelligence used to conduct a drone strike outside the Afghan theater. See *Noor Khan* v. *Secretary of State for Foreign and Commonwealth Affairs* (2014). The German federal courts are currently considering whether the death of a German citizen in an alleged U.S. drone strike was conducted with the help of mobile phone data provided by the German Government. See Louise Osborne, "Germany Denies Phone Data Sent to NSA Used in Drone Attacks," The Guardian, Aug. 12, 2013. See also Frederik Rosen, "Extremely Stealthy and Incredibly Close: Drones, Control and Legal Responsibility," J. Confl. Secur. Law 24 (2013) ("The rapidly growing surveillance capacity of drone technology combined with ever more sophisticated armed capabilities may suggest a capability for exercising a degree of control and authority over territories and persons that may trigger the extraterritorial application of the European Convention of Human Rights.").

[69] See Robert S. Mueller III, "Defeating Terrorism Through Partnerships, Fed. Bur. of Inves." (2008).

The CHAIRMAN. General Mukasey.

STATEMENT OF HON. MICHAEL B. MUKASEY, PARTNER, DEBEVOISE & PLIMPTON, FORMER ATTORNEY GENERAL OF THE UNITED STATES, NEW YORK, NY

Mr. MUKASEY. Mr. Chairman, first of all, thank you for holding this hearing, thank you for hearing me and having me here as part of the process.

I did submit a brief statement. I do not want to duplicate what is in it, because this hearing has developed certain questions that I think are on your mind, on the minds of the rest of the members, and that I probably ought to address those rather than simply go off on my own oration.

With respect to the questions that you posed to the other witnesses at the beginning: Is the AUMF—I think words you used were "broken, obsolete, inadequate"? I am not sure what broken means in this context, but obsolete and inadequate, for sure. I think that the nature of the threat that we face now is essentially the same as the nature of the threat we faced on and before 9/11, even though we may not have been fully aware of it before 9/11, and that is that there are people who are committed, as a matter of religious belief, so they say, to destroy Western civilization, and we are the principal focus of their energies and their activities, although we are not the only focus. We could declare, tomorrow, that the war was over, we could repeal the AUMF, we could repeal every enabling piece of legislation that we have, and that would not change their agenda. They get a vote in this. And I think that it is unrealistic for us to talk about simply taking a statute off the books, as if that, in fact, would change facts on the ground.

I do think, however, that the AUMF can, and should, be changed. In what ways? It names—it does name particular entities; it names al-Qaeda, it names the Taliban, it talks about associated groups and groups that are working in concert with them. What that has necessitated, as you saw, to some extent, with the testimony of the prior witnesses, is some degree of somersaults to find out whether this organization or that organization is or is not associated, is or is not supporting al-Qaeda as it has been identified? I think, rather than doing that, you could come up with a list of organizations, come up with a set of goals that those organizations pursue in common, and then, in very much the same way that the State Department puts groups on the lists of foreign terrorist organizations, have a consultative process involving the State Department, the Defense Department, the Justice Department, and Homeland Security to include entities that, whether they are directly associated, or not, are pursuing the same goal that we know generated the attacks of 9/11 and attacks before that, that Congress would then maintain an ongoing involvement with that process and could examine the legitimacy of having groups on that list, or not, and could examine what steps had to be taken.

Detention authority is not even mentioned in the AUMF and, as I understand it, is simply a derivative authority from the existence of a war. I think we ought to provide for detention authority in a straightforward way, determining who, how, and under what circumstances.

And I am happy to answer your questions.

[The prepared statement of Mr. Mukasey follows:]

Prepared Statement of Michael B. Mukasev

First, I would like to thank the committee, through its chairman and its ranking member, for addressing an issue vital to the security of this country—namely, whether the Authorization for the Use of Military Force (AUMF), passed in the days following the attacks of September 11, 2001, still provides all the authority necessary to protect us. And thank you as well for the privilege of testifying on this subject.

The AUMF, as you will recall, authorized the President to "use all necessary and appropriate force against those nations, organizations, or persons he determines planned, authorized, committed or aided the terrorist attacks that occurred on September 11, 2001, or harbored such organizations or persons. . . ." Upon passage of the AUMF, all three branches of government understood that language to authorize force against al-Qaeda—the organization that planned and carried out those attacks, and the Taliban, the organization that once controlled Afghanistan and harbored al-Qaeda. The power to detain prisoners is not specified anywhere in the AUMF; it has been read into the statute as an implied power of the sort incident to a war.

Events since September 11, 2001, including successes of two administrations in combating both al-Qaeda and the Taliban, have made the AUMF not only obsolete, but dangerously so; future events—including the current administration's decision to cease the war in Afghanistan by mid-December 2014—threaten to make it even more irrelevant.

What has been referred to colloquially as core al-Qaeda has been diminished, and the Taliban no longer formally control Afghanistan. However, other groups loosely related to al-Qaeda, or having the same goals, have sprung up across a broad arc of countries stretching from Asia to Africa, and perhaps in Latin America as well. Some call themselves al-Qaeda—for example, Al Qaeda in the Arabian Peninsula and Al Qaeda in the Islamic Maghreb; others do not—for example, Ansar al-Sharia in Libya and the al-Nusra Front in Syria. Their effects have been seen in conduct as diverse as the attack that killed our Ambassador and three others in Benghazi, in plots to set off bombs in New York's subways and in Times Square. They are inspired by a common ideology that claims to find authority in the Quran. That claim is one that will have to be resolved by Muslims, but Western civilization in general, and the United States in particular, is the focus of that ideology and it is not going away any time soon. Simply saying that there is no war will not fend off the violence generated by that ideology any more than the absence of a state of war before September 2001 prevented the attacks of 9/11.

In spite of the actual or potential lethality of these groups, it becomes increasingly difficult to identify them with any certainty as "affiliates" or "supporters" of al-Qaeda, and we find ourselves going through increasingly fanciful contortions in order to fit them within the definitions in the AUMF so as to permit action to be taken against them.

There are some who have suggested that we can rely on the authority inherent in Article II's grant of "the executive power"—all of it, to the President, to authorize any response to these people and groups. Even if that authority is sufficient to permit a President to act in an emergency, I think there is no way it can be sufficient politically to permit long-term action. I believe that a basis in legislation is necessary to confer that kind of political authority.

Although it might be possible to define the conduct of these groups in a comprehensive yet precise enough way to permit the President to act, there are bound to be close decisions to be made, and I do not think it is politically wise or even possible simply to delegate to the President the authority to determine who does and who does not fit the statutory definition.

As others have, I urge the committee to consider and send to Congress legislation that would designate some groups that we know about, and create a mechanism for designating others, perhaps in the way that the Secretary of State now designates groups as Foreign Terrorist Organizations, through a group drawn from the Departments of State, Defense, Justice, and Homeland Security. I am certainly no fan of sunset provisions, and I do not believe that there is any sunset provision in any authority that inspires our enemies. However, I recognize that it may be politically difficult to authorize an open ended use of force, particularly when the people and groups against whom it is used may expand with time. Accordingly I recommend that a rational but limited deadline be established—perhaps 10 years—beyond which the authority would expire unless extended.

You may also wish to address related issues, including criteria for targeting drone strikes against U.S. citizens abroad away from the battlefield and a requirement that at least the number of such strikes and the estimated number of victims, both intentional and collateral, be reported.

These suggestions subsume many issues and invite many questions, and I would be happy to explore those issues and attempt to answer some of those questions in my oral testimony. Again, I am grateful to the committee for allowing me to participate in its important work.

The CHAIRMAN. Well, thank you.

Thank you both very much.

Let me go to—ask you both of—one of the first questions I asked the previous panel. What does the 9/11 AUMF provide the President, in terms of authorities to use force, that he does not already possess in other authorities?

Mr. KOH. So, Senator, I think a point that did not clearly emerge is, there are two states of affairs. One is armed conflict. When we are in an armed conflict with an organized group that is of a certain intensity and duration, as a matter of law, it is easier to conduct that ongoing struggle until you reach a point where they are defeated. And certainly, on September 19, 2001, we were in that state of affairs. You had al-Qaeda, the Taliban, and associated forces. That went on, and many major actions were taken as part of an armed conflict.

At a certain point—and this is what Jay Johnson called the "tipping point"—you could say that that group has, essentially, been defeated. They may not surrender, but, at that point, they are less of an organized group than they are a set of threats. And when you have that set of threats and you consider them a continuing imminent threat, you can get rid of the belt and go with the suspenders, which is the authority to respond to those continuing imminent threats in self-defense against known attackers.

And the question is, When do you do that? You have to do it when the situation on the ground permits. So, you were giving the example of Iraq. It may well be that now, several years after all troops are withdrawn, is a good time to withdraw the AUMF authority; where it might not have been, in the last days of the drawdown, when there were still American soldiers there.

So, that is the key; we have a belt-and-suspenders system, but the armed-conflict scenario works best when you are in an ongoing armed conflict with an organized, armed group and you need to be using targeting and detention on a very regular basis. That does not fit well into the sporadic threat scenario.

The CHAIRMAN. But, my question still prevails, in trying to get a greater clarity of answer. Could the President have—conduct and continue to conduct all activities that he has—being conducted, absent an AUMF of 9/11?

Mr. KOH. Well, I do not—I am no longer part of the information flow on the threat stream. My view is that some parts of al-Qaeda have been pretty much subdued, other parts are still very active— AQAP, AQIM. And then there are other entities which are dangerous, but they are not going to attack the homeland and they are not part of al-Qaeda and they do not fall under the AUMF. However, they do present continuing and imminent threats. For example, the Benghazi attackers. So, you have the legal authority to respond to them, even without an AUMF.

The CHAIRMAN. General Mukasey, do you have a view?

Mr. MUKASEY. I think part of it was responded to before—the AUMF does override the War Powers Act. And so, any action taken would not have to be reported under the War Powers Act. In addition, it provides a coordinating mechanism for responses. Yes, there is Article 2 authority for the President to respond to imminent threats. But, evaluating imminence, as was pointed out before, can be an elusive process, particularly when obviously we are not privy to the plans of terrorists. They do not tell us precisely when they are going to act, they do not tell us, necessarily, even what, precisely, they are planning. But, once they are identified as a terrorist organization, it is, I think, rational, at least, to consider members of those organizations, and the organizations themselves, to constitute imminent threats, unless there is good evidence to the contrary.

The CHAIRMAN. The previous panel suggested, I think, by their testimony, that, absent the AUMF, Article 2 provisions would give the President all the authorities that he needed to continue to conduct those operations. Almost seemed like it was superfluous to have an AUMF. Is that a view that you share? And if not, what is the difference, in your view?

Mr. KOH. So, Senator, a little history of the kind that Senator Durbin recalled, I think is helpful. On September 11, the Nation was shocked, people wanted the President to respond with all available tools. He could invoke his Article 2 authority, but Congress gave him a very broad statutory authority, as well. But, it was supposed to be against those people who were responsible for September 11 and to prevent a future September 11.

In the last administration, these two rationales were merged. Constitutional authority was invoked all the time, the AUMF was used in a very broad way. There was a lot of objection to that. At the beginning of this administration—at this point, we were in the middle of habeas litigation, et cetera—the Justice Department offered a narrowing interpretation of the AUMF, and the Obama administration shifted to the AUMF as the main basis for its activities. It rejected the notion that there was a Global War on Terror, but said that there was a war against al-Qaeda, the Taliban, and associated forces that was not limited to just one country, but it was not limited—it was not the whole world, either. And the net result of that is, there has been more of a convergence on the legal rationales.

A year ago, the President, at the NDU, not only gave a speech setting forth the standards, but signed Presidential policy guidance specifying those standards. So, I think we are now operating in a world in which the President's power is, by his own statement, much more constrained. And he stated that his long-term goal is to bring the war to an end.

The CHAIRMAN. So, based upon your answer, if the AUMF was repealed and the President, as you described, relying upon that AUMF for action, would either have to cease such activities or he would then have to turn to his—to make his Article 2 claims.

Mr. KOH. Well, let me just make a hypothetical situation. If the President thought he needed to make 100 more strikes against al-Qaeda to defeat them, it would be very unwise to eliminate the AUMF. If he thought that the core of al-Qaeda has been defeated, that al-Qaeda—those remnants might occasionally strike, that would be a moment in which it would be safe to move for repeal of AUMF authority and rely on self-defense authorities, going forward. In other words, the self-defense arguments are not all-purpose alternatives.

Finally, if Congress wanted to codify the self-defense authorities in a more limited way, that would be a narrowing of the AUMF. And, to my mind, that would be more appropriate for a situation in which there were fewer need to attack or detain al-Qaeda, the Taliban, or associated forces.

The CHAIRMAN. What would happen to the government's legal authority to continue to detain prisoners at Guantanamo if, hypothetically, the 2001 AUMF were repealed?

Mr. KOH. Well, again, Senator, it would depend on how many people were there. If there are 150 people or so, if those who are in Yemen have been moved to Yemen pursuant to negotiations that are apparently going on, if those who are Taliban had moved off, if you are talking about a small group of people, some of those individuals might be still detainable under criminal detention authorities, some of them might be detainable under immigration detention authorities, some of them might have to be dealt with by new legislation considered by you. But, that would be, at that point, a very small number of people, say 30 people as opposed to 150 people.

The CHAIRMAN. Regardless of the size, what is the legal authority if the AUMF is repealed? What is the legal authority to detain people at Guantanamo?

Mr. KOH. Well, we just have to remember, Senator, that the AUMF is belligerent combatant authority, authority to use necessary and appropriate force against belligerent combatants. Individuals may not be detainable as belligerent combatants, but they may be criminals, they may have committed immigration violations, they may be subject to other forms of civilian detention. And you have to evaluate that on an individualized basis.

The CHAIRMAN. But, civilian detention in a place like Guantanamo?

Mr. KOH. My understanding is that the goal would be to move people off of Guantanamo. But, this is, to me, akin to the question—if you are trying to bail out a boat, you worry about the last 4 inches of water when you get there. I think the main challenge now is to bring the numbers in Guantanamo down by moving off people who can be transferred, by moving off people——

The CHAIRMAN. I would disagree——

Mr. KOH [continuing]. Through negotiations——

The CHAIRMAN [continuing]. Insofar as that there is a broader essence of policy of what is the legal authority to maintain people in a place like Guantanamo, whether 150 are there and tomorrow there will be a different Guantanamo. And that is what I was trying to——

Mr. KOH. So, Senator Menendez, the Justice Department, last week, issued a report, in response to a congressional mandate, which described the legal authorities that would be used if individuals were brought from Guantanamo to the United States. And I think they would be anticipating a relatively small number at the point in which that would be exercised. They argued there are various legal authorities. I think you would have to engage them to see whether you agree.

The CHAIRMAN. Senator Corker.

Senator CORKER. Thank you, Mr. Chairman.

And thank you both for being here.

It seems to me that the description of "imminent threat" is one that, over time, needs to be teased out. I mean, do you guys agree that imminent threat is one that can evolve, determined—based on what someone actually wants to do and, really, is difficult to define?

Mr. KOH. I think the term that is being used is "continuing and imminent threat," which is even a narrower set of people. So, we know what an imminent threat is, Senator. You know, a guy gets on a plane wearing underwear in his bomb—a bomb in his underwear or in his sneakers, and the next thing to do is to launch the attack. That is an imminent threat.

But, if you have an organization which is repeatedly planning attacks, and sometimes they use underwear bombs, sometimes they use shoes, sometimes they use cartridges, sometimes they use something in Times Square, the need to act against them may come earlier, because they never use the same delivery mechanism twice. I mean, they will not fly a plane into the Twin Towers——

Senator CORKER. And I think the point you make about that type of threat is, certainly, really clear. But, my guess is, if we get into a classified setting and discuss these things, there are numbers of groups that the administration has determined that are under, you know, this imminent-threat issue, and, you know—I do not know, AQAP, I do not know, are they planning threats against us today? ISIS, in Syria, are they—right now, they have their hands full. My guess is, at some point they may well do that. But, if we determined that they were an imminent threat——

Mr. KOH. Senator——

Senator CORKER [continuing]. I think that would be an interesting——

Mr. KOH [continuing]. Your question——

Senator CORKER. Is that not an interesting question to you?

Mr. KOH. You have looked at this intelligence and in——

Senator CORKER. No, I have not looked at intelligence. I want to make sure any intelligence people watching—I have not looked at the intelligence. I am just basing my question off the last witness.

Mr. KOH. In general terms, the primary factors are whether they attacked us before, whether they had success in that, and whether they are planning to attack us again in the very near future, and whether all signs leave no innocent explanation for that. That is an imminent threat.

Senator CORKER. And to the question that Mr. Preston raised earlier about Afghanistan and getting back to the fact that the administration has not called this a Global War on Terror, but has—you know, is certainly carrying out counterterrorist operations all around the globe, if Afghanistan winds down at some point—let us say 24 months from now we do not have people doing what they now, today, are doing—would there need to be an AUMF to continue to strike entities that, you know, could pose a threat to us down the road? And I would like both of you to answer that, if you would.

Mr. KOH. Unfortunately, there are many terrorist networks. But, you can distinguish two kinds: those who want to attack us—attack our buildings, attack our people, attack our soil—and those who are just dangerous or have local aspirations, and they may not like us. Now, the latter group are not members of al-Qaeda, we are not at war with them; and we may not like them and they may not like us, but we have to keep them under surveillance. The group that we care about are those who would attack the homeland and who pose a continuing and imminent threat of doing so, and where you think that there is a very good likelihood, because they did it before.

Senator CORKER. Mr. Mukasey.

Mr. MUKASEY. The standard is continuing imminent threat. I think where I part company, to a certain extent, with Professor Koh is the characterization of some of the local groups as people who, "do not like us." It is much more than that. They are people who have this attacking our homeland figuratively on their list of things to do on the refrigerator in the morning, if they had refrigerators. So, I think I would be somewhat more generous in my definition. But, yes, it has to be a continuing imminent threat, and one that can be rationally interpreted as continuing imminent threat.

Senator CORKER. And so—but, let me come back. I mean, if we end the actual physical operations that we have ongoing in Afghanistan, I know there may be covert activities that would not as Murphy pointed out earlier, may not be defined under these—but, would we need to continue to have an AUMF of any kind to continue our fight against, not the Global War on Terror, per this administration, but terror that happens all around the world?

Mr. MUKASEY. As a legal matter, there is at least one vote in Hamdi that says that we need it in order to detain. But, more broadly—and I know the last group was cautioned to stay away from policy, but this does trench into policy—we need some kind of backing from Congress in order for the country to be behind any effort that we make. And that is true regardless of where we do it.

Senator CORKER. But, I do not think Mr. Koh agrees with that.

Mr. KOH. Well, I agree with your view, Senator, that Congress has a role to play in defining how much authority it wants the President to have to deal with the current situation. And the current situation, it seems to me, is one where if the organizations with which we have been in armed conflict for the last 13 years are reduced in danger, you could shrink the AUMF to address their remnants or, at a certain point, when you think that they are a sporadic threat, you could eliminate the AUMF altogether and rely on continuing and imminent threat. But, that would allow you, for example, it seems to me, to have legal authority to—as an imminent threat, deal with the people who killed our citizens in Benghazi. They did it before, they pose a continuing imminent threat, they seem to raise those issues. Now, there would be things that would need to be done. If the Libyan Government is capable of addressing them, you might have to defer to that first.

Senator CORKER. Mr. Chairman, thank you.

And thank you both for being here.

The CHAIRMAN. Senator Murphy.

Senator MURPHY. Thank you, Mr. Chairman.

Mr. Koh, I really appreciate your suggestions on how Congress can grapple with this expanded Article 2 authority, especially in perhaps the future absence of an AUMF.

I guess you hear that one of the questions—this is a question for General Mukasey, as well—you hear that we have twin struggles here. We have a struggle with what authority we grant the President, and then we have a struggle with what role, then, Congress plays to oversee that authority. And part of the danger that I see is that, as more and more potential activities happen under covert authorities, there is a very small group of Senators and Congressmen that actually get to oversee those questions of what is an imminent threat. There is a tiny, select group of people who have jurisdiction and clearance in order to determine whether there is or is not an imminent threat that would trigger those Article 2 authorities.

I would love to get rid of AUMF, but my concern is that we then live in a world in which the determination of imminent threat and the factors that go into that are available to be debated by a very small number of Senators and Congressmen. And, given how fuzzy the first panel suggested the limitations on that authority are, reserving the authority, as I heard it, to take action against a sovereign nation without consulting Congress first, what is both your recommendations on how we provide for a more robust and open debate in Congress about the specifics relative to authorities under Article 2?

Mr. KOH. So, Senator, your questions, I think, illustrate the—how to—what is the relationship between constitutional authority of the President and statutory authority of the Congress. And maybe the best way to think of it is what we call "framework statutes." There is a constitutional space in which the President can act. And if he acted under constitutional authority, it would not be illegal, but he has no guidance. And so, in many areas of the law—intelligence oversight, international emergencies, sanctions, arms export control—Congress has passed, essentially, framework legislation that defines what can or cannot be done, defines reporting requirements, defines who is supposed to be part of the process, and clarifies what some of these issues mean. For example, it could clarify what "continuing and imminent threat" means.

Now, the reason why it is important to put it this way is, if that statute suddenly disappeared, would the President still have authority? As a constitutional matter, probably, yes. But, would that be the best policy, as opposed to working with Congress to be what they called in the "Steel Seizure Case," category 1, the highest level of legitimacy? Clearly, it is better for Congress to have framed this constitutional space and then for the President to operate pursuant to these rules, both the restrictions as well as getting the authorities.

Senator MURPHY. General Mukasey, do you see a policy danger in a limited number of Members of Congress being involved in these discussions about Article 2 authority in the absence of AUMF?

Mr. MUKASEY. Of a statute?

Senator MURPHY. Yes.

Mr. MUKASEY. Absolutely. And I think you put your finger on a good reason for not simply letting the AUMF lapse or get off the books, but, rather, reshaping it, doing some of what Professor Koh suggested, maybe some of what I suggested before. You have—because if you have a statute on the books, then this committee, the Intelligence Committees, the Armed Services Committee can conduct their oversight functions in addition to having particular Members of Congress briefed, and—a limited number of Members of Congress briefed, and have that information restricted to only a few people.

Senator MURPHY. And I think the claim that many of us is—have made is that, as we have seen broadened the authority to conduct activities under Article 2, to conduct ongoing large-scale military activities in a covert manner, it becomes more problematic to not have the Foreign Relations Committee and the Foreign Affairs Committee read into those matters, because they have broad and sometimes crippling foreign policy implications for the United States. I think it is a worthwhile endeavor.

I want to just follow up on some questions that the chairman was asking the first panel specific to the authority on operations in Syria. I am not sure that we got—I think the answer was—is that there was authority for the President to conduct military operations in Syria, as was initially proposed, without congressional authorization. I was not particularly clear as to where that authority would have come from. But, let me just ask that to both of you.

Do you believe that the President had authority, should he have decided independently to take military action in Syria, as he had proposed and asked Congress for authority, without congressional authorization?

Mr. KOH. So, I think it depends on what he would have done. If what he did was simply hit a bunch of chemical weapons sites, and that was a one-time thing, we would be hard-pressed to say that was unconstitutional.

The question, as a matter of law, is, Is it war, in a constitutional sense? If it is war, Congress has to approve it. A one-time hit on a bunch of chemical weapons may not rise to the level. If it goes on for 60 days, then, under the War Powers Resolution, the question is, Is it hostilities, in a statutory sense? And, contrary to what Senator Corker said, the setting up of the no-fly zone happened in 10 days. Sixty days on, less than 1 percent of the ordnance in Kosovo was being dropped in Libya. My view was then, and remains, that it was not hostilities, in a statutory sense.

I want to come back to one point, Senator, which I think is important. I think Congress has three options. One bad option, which I would urge you not to pursue, which is to use a sense of frustration with the AUMF to expand it and extend it inadvertently. I think that would perpetuate war. I think you have two good options, or two better options than that. One is, if you want to narrow it to meet the current situation, and then ultimately repeal it, that is the best. If this is not a good time to legislate because people cannot agree, you could see whether the situation on the ground leads to the eventual diminishing of the threat of al-Qaeda, and just repeal it later. In other words, not narrow, but just move right to the repeal later on down the road.

But, I think that is the real choice. Do not extend and expand. Either wait and repeal or narrow and repeal.

Senator MURPHY. I know we have a vote on the floor, so I will yield back at this point.

The CHAIRMAN. Okay.

Well, with the thanks, to both of you, of the committee for your insights—and I have a feeling we will be continually seeking to engage you in the days ahead—the record for this hearing will be held open until the close of business on Friday.

And, with that, this hearing is adjourned.

[Whereupon, at 12:28 p.m., the hearing was adjourned.]

———————

ADDITIONAL MATERIAL SUBMITTED FOR THE RECORD

WRITTEN STATEMENT OF HUMAN RIGHTS FIRST

SUMMARY AND RECOMMENDATIONS

Human Rights First welcomes the Senate Foreign Relations Committee's attention to the status and future of the 2001 Authorization for the Use of Military Force (AUMF). The debate at hand raises profound legal and policy issues that are critical to our democracy and our security. Is the United States engaged in armed conflict as defined by international law? If so, does the 2001 AUMF meet domestic and international legal criteria for authorizing the types of use of force that the U.S. is now employing?

These questions may seem inessential at best to policymakers and operators intent on securing authorization to go after a suspect or push an interrogation in real time. And they may seem academic or a luxury when placed against the lives of comrades lost on the battlefield in Afghanistan, or the fate of 200 girls ripped from school into sexual servitude.

In fact, the strong wall between war and peace underpins the democratic stability that Boko Haram wants to keep out of Nigeria and Osama bin Laden sought to undermine here at home. A state of perpetual warfare skews our policymaking framework toward decisions designed to eliminate—rather than manage—threats, an unrealistic goal that leads to unbalanced and unhealthy policy results. The longer the United States remains in a state of armed conflict to take advantage of the flexibility war allows, the more likely it is that extraordinary powers become the norm and, in the worst case, that policies creep in that are the hallmarks of dictatorships and enemies of human rights: detentions without charge or trial, extrajudicial killings, military tribunals, and mass surveillance.

In recent years, military and diplomatic leaders have documented the high increasing costs of prolonged and global armed conflict: partners and allies reluctant to cooperate on counterterrorism operations, authoritarian leaders cynically pointing to U.S. excesses to justify their own repressive policies, loss of support and trust in American efforts among publics in countries such as Yemen. At home as well, public controversy and distrust has risen around every aspect of our wartime activities. And counterterrorism professionals continue to point to a suite of core competencies—nonmilitary policies that are essential to our security—that are underemphasized and underresourced.

To date, Congress, military leaders, and outside experts have debated reforms and transparency piecemeal. Below, Human Rights First reviews the legal and policy ramifications of maintaining the current AUMF, adopting a new one, or moving to reliance on nonwar national security authorities, and makes the following recommendations:

- Congress and the administration should publicly debate and clarify the shifting nature of the threat posed by Al Qaeda, and the core competencies and additional legal authorities, if any, needed to keep Americans secure.
- The administration should remedy the lack of transparency about current U.S. policy under the AUMF, by disclosing to Congress and the American people:
    - Æ With which groups the administration considers the United States to be at war;
    - Æ Which groups the administration considers to be "associated forces";
    - Æ The countries in which military force is currently being used, the criteria it uses to classify targets and collateral damage; and
    - Æ Any and all legal memoranda and policy guidance that govern lethal targeting operations.
- The administration should describe in concrete and specific terms the conditions necessary to bring an end to the armed conflict with Al Qaeda and associated forces.
- The administration should clarify and reform its legal and policy framework for the use of lethal force outside of active zones of hostilities to put it on more solid footing by bringing it further in line with the requirements of international human rights law.
- Congress should hold a series of hearings, with the cooperation of the administration, to examine the most effective way to narrow and ultimately repeal the 2001 AUMF. Congress should not pass any new AUMF that would expand the mandate contained within the 2001 AUMF.
- The administration and Congress should seek and implement a bipartisan solution to remove one of the most problematic legacies of the AUMF—the detention

facilities at Guantanamo Bay—by transferring all cleared detainees to their home or third countries, prosecuting detainees suspected of criminal conduct in Article III courts, and transferring the remaining detainees to the United States with a view toward their ultimate release or prosecution elsewhere.

INTRODUCTION

Is war the best way for the government to organize, and citizens to understand, a campaign that reflects few of the attributes of how we understood war for hundreds of years?

The law has much to say about this; America's best lawyers and soldiers believed a clear separation between wartime and peacetime behavior was essential, and worked to codify it in our laws and international law.

This hearing has as its starting point a legal debate: is the United States engaged in armed conflict as defined by international law? If so, does the 2001 AUMF meet domestic and international legal criteria for authorizing the types of use of force that the U.S. is now employing?

These questions may seem inessential at best to policymakers and operators intent on securing authorization to go after a suspect or push an interrogation in real time. And they may seem academic or a luxury when placed against the lives of comrades lost on the battlefield in Afghanistan, or the fate of 200 girls ripped from school into sexual servitude.

In fact, the strong wall between war and peace underpins the democratic stability that Boko Haram seeks to keep out of Nigeria and Osama bin Laden sought to undermine here at home. A state of perpetual warfare skews our policymaking framework toward decisions designed to eliminate—rather than manage—threats, an unrealistic goal that leads to unbalanced and unhealthy policy results. The longer the United States remains in a state of armed conflict to take advantage of the flexibility war allows, the more likely it is that extraordinary powers become the norm and, in the worst case, that policies creep in that are the hallmarks of dictatorships and enemies of human rights: detentions without charge or trial, extrajudicial killings, military tribunals, and mass surveillance.

Congress, military leaders, and outside experts have debated such reforms piecemeal, out of concern for fundamental rights and freedoms and a sense that U.S. counterterrorism efforts are warped by an overemphasis on tools available in wartime.

Course correction must come with limiting the scope of the government's claimed armed conflict to situations that actually resemble war—the exchange of hostilities of sufficient intensity between the United States and another state or an organized armed group. They can begin when the administration sets out clearly where and against whom it believes the United States to be in an armed conflict, and works with Congress to decide whether such authority is the wisest choice to achieve its objectives. The United States clearly remains in an armed conflict in Afghanistan. However, counterterrorism operations far from any battlefield against groups that have limited to no connection to core Al Qaeda or the Taliban and the 9/11 attacks do not fall within an armed conflict framework, unless the facts on the ground meet the legal test for what constitutes an armed conflict under international law: ongoing hostilities of sufficient intensity with an organized armed group. Sporadic acts of violence or terrorist attacks by groups or individuals do not meet this test.

Despite the best efforts of intelligence and security agencies, the United States will likely continue to face threats from terrorism, which may result in successful terrorist attacks such as the attacks against our Embassy in Benghazi on September 11, 2012. The response, however, cannot and should not be to declare war or authorize the use of military force against any terrorist group that presents a concern to the United States. To do so would not only be inconsistent with the fundamental principles of the rule of law, but would also likely be ineffective in the long-term struggle against extremist groups that seek to goad the U.S. into overreaction.

WHAT IS THE AUMF?

Three days after the unprecedented attacks of September 11, 2001, Congress passed the most open-ended Authorization for the Use of Military Force (AUMF) in American history. This law's key 60-word sentence granted then-President George W. Bush power to use "all necessary and appropriate force against those nations, organizations, or persons" that he determined either executed the attacks or aided those who did.[1]

The AUMF does not specify whom its mandate is directed against, or what military objectives would satisfy the mandate. Perhaps consequently, in the nearly 13 years since its passage, the AUMF has been invoked not only to conduct the war in Afghanistan but also to justify targeted killings under the drone program reaching from Somalia to Yemen and the prolonged detention without charge of prisoners in Guantanamo Bay and Bagram Air Field. It has contributed to a wartime climate enabling expanded government powers such as the PATRIOT Act and the NSA's expansive domestic surveillance programs.

WHY REVISIT IT

The 2001 AUMF was passed by Congress within days of the 9/11 attacks, before the Bush administration had identified with certainty the full universe of those perpetrators.

As the Obama administration prepares to end combat operations in Afghanistan, numerous legal authorities have called into question the continued viability of the AUMF. The Supreme Court stated of the AUMF in *Hamdi* v. *Rumsfeld* that "If the practical circumstances of a given conflict are entirely unlike those of the conflicts that informed the development of the law of war, that understanding [of who may be detained until the cessation of hostilities] may unravel." [2] This concern has been echoed by Brigadier General Mark Martins,[3] chief prosecutor for the military commission trials at Guantanamo Bay, and former Pentagon General Counsel Jeh Johnson,[4] now Secretary of Homeland Security.

The 2001 AUMF is, on paper, confined to organizations responsible for committing or helping with the 9/11 attacks, or others who harbored them—generally understood to be core Al Qaeda, the group directly led by Ayman al-Zawahiri, and the Taliban in Afghanistan, and other groups directly engaged in hostilities with the United States. The administration has officially interpreted those organizations to include Al Qaeda and "associated forces," including groups such as Al Qaeda in the Arabian Peninsula (AQAP), even though groups such as AQAP have little to no connection to the 9/11 attacks.

Terrorist organizations in the headlines today, and groups that now pose specific, credible threats to the United States, often have a loose or unclear connection to "core Al Qaeda" and the 9/11 attackers. Security professionals from across the political spectrum have commented that the 2001 AUMF bears little relevance to the shape of the struggle against terrorist groups that the U.S. remains engaged in.

At least as important, the greatly varying tactics and levels of competence and ambition of our adversaries do not lend themselves to the set of rules and policies set aside in law as "armed conflict," or the all-or-nothing approach evoked for Americans by the word "war."

"Armed Conflict" is no longer the most effective paradigm for U.S. counterterrorism policy

An overreliance on our military does a disservice to the extraordinary economic, diplomatic, and human capital resources that the United States can marshal in support of policy goals. Moreover, pursuing an unachievable goal of complete security, contributing to an inability to contextualize threats appropriately and deploy a full range of counterterrorism strategies short of war-making contributes to a dangerous stagnation in the foreign policy making apparatus of the U.S. Government.

Shifting away from the authorities created by the overstretching of the 2001 AUMF is the first step in reforming U.S. counterterrorism policy. By continuing institutional development of core competencies and acknowledging the shifting nature of the Al Qaeda threat, the U.S. Government can move from the post-September 11 framework to a more nuanced and flexible approach to protecting our security. Given how our adversaries have evolved, where the existing approach has succeeded and where it has failed, such a shift will be more effective. Winding down controversial wartime activities will free resources and attention to remake our security assistance, promote security sector reform, the rule of law and democracy, and innovate in economic approaches. Those are changes that will ensure the United States can marshal its full military, economic, and human capital resources for ongoing efforts to thwart the tactics and perpetrators of terrorism.

The large-scale wars in Iraq and Afghanistan conducted under the AUMF have carried a heavy price tag for the U.S. military, particularly on equipment, personnel, and veterans. The Department of Defense can anticipate an extremely large price tag for the withdrawal of military forces from Afghanistan, and even more costly will be the replenishing of obsolete or defective equipment. Linda J. Bilmes writes that "equipment, material, vehicles and other fixed assets have depreciated at an estimated six times the peacetime rate, due to heavy utilization, poor repair and upkeep in the field, and the harsh conditions in the region." [5] In 2008 testimony to the Senate Armed Services Committee, General Richard Cody drew attention to the wars' effects on readiness, arguing that because of heavy deployments, soldiers and marines lacked training for major combat operations using their entire range of weapons. In this testimony, Cody stated that the Army did not have fully ready combat brigades on standby should another threat or conflict occur.[6] At a time of tight budgets, and national debate over how to meet our obligations to the members of our Armed Forces and maintain readiness for tomorrow's security threats, an existing AUMF which would permit a return to large-scale combat, and encourage the flow of resources into military counterterrorism as opposed to other policy options, is not in the Nation's interest.

As a world leader that promotes prosperity, opportunity, and liberty, the U.S. should be actively seeking a state of affairs in which armed conflict is minimized and cabined, rather than a permanent state of war with occasional lulls in the fighting.

Asserting that we are entrenched in constant struggle and armed conflict projects to the world a lack of confidence in our ideals and institutions, and it sends the wrong message about the power of our opponents. As George Kennan wrote 68 years ago about another atypical international conflict, the cold war, the central challenge facing the United States was to "create among the peoples of the world generally the impression of a country which knows what it wants, which is coping successfully with the problems of its internal life and with the responsibilities of a world power, and which has a spiritual vitality capable of holding its own among the major ideological currents of the time."[7]

Instead, the continuation of the policies enacted within a war paradigm after 9/11—ramped-up levels of targeted killings, lack of transparency about targets and outcomes, continued questions around rendition, detention, surveillance, detention at Guantanamo and prosecutions by military commission—is damaging our global leadership and credibility on basic human rights and the rule of law.

Simply put, the war-based policies the U.S. has adopted are not popular with our allies or with civilians in the countries where we are engaged in a contest of ideals with extremists, and where the outcome may depend on people's belief that the U.S. is on their side.[8]

The unpopularity of these policies is cynically exploited by those who wish us ill, and those who benefit from the United States diminished influence. Russian President Vladimir Putin, Zimbabwe's Robert Mugabe, Syria's Bashar al-Assad, and Iran's Mahmoud Ahmadinejad have all pointed to Guantanamo to deflect attention from human rights abuses in their own countries. When the U.S. advocates with other governments for respect for human rights, its words are instantly undermined when a newscast sets images of Guantanamo against the American assertions of human rights as universal values.

War-based policies have specific negative consequences for our security. Extremist groups use them to attract recruits; the New York Times has reported that "drones have replaced Guantanamo as the recruiting tool of choice for militants."[9]

These policies also undercut our ability to cooperate with crucial partners and allies. After a U.S. drone strike in Waziristan killed two German citizens in 2011, Germany restricted the type of information it shares with the U.S., a sharp reversal from being an eager partner in America's fight against terrorism.[10]

Our insistence on using military commissions rather than federal courts to prosecute some terrorism suspects has also had negative consequences for the counterterrorism cooperation we depend upon. Attorney General Eric Holder said, "A number of countries have indicated that they will not cooperate with the United States in certain counterterrorism efforts—for instance, in providing evidence or extraditing suspects—if we intend to use that cooperation in pursuit of a military commission prosecution."[11]

AUMF-based military detention policies also continue to have negative ramifications. For example, the administration has stated that Guantanamo, which is based on AUMF authority, "plagues our bilateral and multilateral relationships, creates friction with governments whose nationals we detain, provides cover for regimes whose detention practices we oppose, and provides our enemies with a symbol used to foster anti-U.S. sentiments around the world."[12]

The choices made by Washington within an armed conflict framework are setting precedents that may harm our interests when used by other nations. John Brennan has said of drone use that the United States is "establishing precedents that other nations may follow, and not all of them will be nations that share our interests or the premium we put on protecting human life, including innocent civilians."[13]

WHY NOT LIVE WITH THE EXISTING AUMF?

Many observers have suggested that, either because the existing AUMF has allowed for counterterrorism policies under which no massive attacks on the U.S.

have been repeated, or because a polarized Congress in an election year is ill-suited to deliberate a new framework, the wisest course for the U.S. is to leave matters as they are. We disagree.

First, while concern over the AUMF's validity after withdrawal from the Afghanistan theater is real, the President retains sufficient authority to counter future threats from terrorism without the AUMF, as we lay out below.

With respect to detention, the President and Congress should not allow the issue of Guantanamo to carry forward what has now become the longest war in American history. There is a reasonable path forward to dealing with Guantanamo, and legal experts agree that detainees must be prosecuted or transferred at the end of active hostilities.

Second, the legal framework created by the AUMF is ill-fitting for the current threats we face and does not satisfy human rights advocates, the military, or counterterrorism professionals. Both liberals and conservatives have expressed concerns about the growing disconnect between the authorities and our actions. The further we get from 9/11, there is every reason to expect that the fit will grow more awkward, pushback from our partners sharper, and possibilities for abuse greater.

Finally, standing war authorities are not needed for effective counterterrorism policy, and in some instances prove distorting and counterproductive to keeping Americans safe.

THE U.S. CAN EFFECTIVELY COUNTER TERRORISM WITHOUT IT

Counterterrorism and military leaders agree that a successful U.S. policy will rely far less on the use of force, especially large-scale military engagements and occupations, than was the case in the years immediately following 9/11. From former Afghanistan commanders saying ''we can't bomb our way to victory'' to recent media coverage of the difficulty the CIA is having transitioning away from wartime activities,[14] evidence is mounting that Congress and the administration have much work to do to strengthen a comprehensive approach which leverages economic, diplomatic and human resources as well as intelligence and military assets. Continued emphasis on war authorities and the activities that flow from them has resulted in underdevelopment and underresourcing of some elements of a ''whole-of-government'' approach. The best counterterrorism policy for the post-post-9/11 era will put more resources into these core competencies, resources gained by getting away from the financial and human costs of the war paradigm.

Conditional Security Assistance: The best way to keep America safe is to help partners ensure that terrorist threats are defeated in the countries where they start. This entails strong, effective support for military, intelligence, law enforcement and the rule of law. But too often over the last decade, resources for civilian security assistance have been stretched too thin, while counterterrorism training in Africa, the Middle East and Southeast Asia was carried out by contractors while the best U.S. counterterrorism troops were deployed in Iraq and Afghanistan.

Sustainable Democratic Institutions and the Rule of Law: Funding to support independent strong courts, police, and local governments in countries facing the threat of terrorism has declined more sharply than military spending, while important parts of military assistance, such as vetting counterterrorism units for human rights abuse under the Leahy Law, remain grossly underfunded. The Leahy Law can also be used more robustly to resource and incentivize military justice in partner countries.

Counter Threat Finance as a Tool to Marginalize Extremists: Perhaps Washington's greatest counterterrorism innovation in the post 9/11 years, this approach is most effective when enforced multilaterally under U.S. leadership—which requires international support for U.S. approaches.

Maximize the Role of the Criminal Justice System: More than 500 individuals have been convicted of international terrorism charges in federal court since 9/11.[15]

Improve Effectiveness, Focus of Intelligence Community: Observers continue to report that the intelligence community's transition off a wartime footing is struggling and needs more emphasis from within and oversight from without.

CHALLENGES AND RECOMMENDATIONS

In both his National Defense University (NDU) speech and the 2014 State of the Union Address, President Obama committed to moving the United States away from a permanent war footing, arguing that ''We must define the nature and scope of this struggle, or else it will define us.''[16] His administration has since taken concrete steps toward transparency, oversight, and reform in specific areas including the targeted killing program and domestic surveillance efforts, and reinvigorated efforts to reduce the detainee population at Guantanamo and close the detention facility permanently. Ending reliance on the AUMF and the policies that go with it is crucial to shifting United States counterterrorism policy off of a permanent war footing.

To that end, Human Rights First urges Congress and the administration to work together to develop shared understandings about the shifting nature of the threat posed by terrorism; the current uses of wartime authorities and what they have accomplished; and the framework of an effective, whole-of-government counterterrorism policy that keeps Americans safe while reassuring our citizens and the world that we remain committed to human rights, liberty, and personal freedoms for ourselves and others.

Recognize and clarify the shifting nature of threat

Al Qaeda is no longer the same organization in terms of capability, structure, capacity, or ambition that launched the September 11 attacks against the United States. Policymakers no longer frame the counterterrorism challenge as hunting down a specific group of individuals responsible for specific attacks or protracted troop deployments in the Middle East.

The Al Qaeda core leadership that threatened the United States in the aftermath of the September 11 attacks was the highly centralized critical node of a financial, ideological, and human capital terrorist network. This node has since been vastly reduced in terms of capability and influence. As then-Secretary of Defense Leon Panetta said in 2012, "over the last few years, Al Qaeda's leadership ranks have been decimated. This includes the loss of four of Al Qaeda's five top leaders in the last 2½ years alone—Osama bin Laden, Sheikh Saeed al-Masri, Atiyah Abd al-Rahman, and Abu Yahya al-Libi." [17]

What has emerged in its wake is a complex web of groups, sharing at minimum an attraction to terrorist violence and a desire to trade on the Al Qaeda "brand." Some, such as al-Nusra, have explicitly sworn allegiance to Al Qaeda's core leadership and take direction from bin Laden's successor, Ayman al-Zawahiri; [18] others appear to receive some training or financial support but limit their aims to internal or regional struggles, unlike Al Qaeda (Boko Haram appears to fit in this category); [19] and some have little or no operational connection or, as is the case of the Islamic State of Iraq and Greater Syria (ISIS, previously known as Al Qaeda in Iraq), have been thrown out of the Al Qaeda family." [20]

The AUMF categories of 9/11 perpetrators, supporters, or associated groups thus lack relevance to the current challenge. Specific groups, be they legitimate "franchises" of Al Qaeda core or merely imitators, must be assessed individually on the basis of their capabilities and ambitions, which vary significantly.

It is misleading to characterize the rise of these other groups—connected in varying degrees or not at all to core Al Qaeda—as more or even equally dangerous to the United States. President Obama remarked that "in the years to come, not every collection of thugs that labels themselves Al Qaeda will pose a credible threat to the United States." [21]

Many pose an intense threat to their home governments and regional stability—in some cases American allies. Many, such as Boko Haram, ISIS, and al-Nusra have carried out large-scale attacks on civilians. Their rise must not be a matter of indifference to Americans.

But that does not mean that a war footing—in legal terms, an armed conflict authorized by an AUMF—is the right policy response to most or all of them. It is simple logic that as Al Qaeda has changed, so must the U.S. response. By failing to recognize that many groups seeking to use the Al Qaeda label or connection for their own prestige do not constitute an imminent threat to the United States, we provide an overblown excuse to use far-reaching wartime policies that breed resentment in the international community and put our most fundamental rights and principles in jeopardy.

Enable intelligent debate by clarifying for Americans where our Nation is using AUMF authorities and with what results

Discussion of where armed conflict authorities are or are not needed is greatly hampered by the fact that the American people and many Members of Congress do not know basic facts about what operations are currently conducted under the AUMF, what other authorities are used to underpin uses of force, and what the results are. To gauge the costs and benefits of war authorities versus other authorities, enact new laws or repeal existing provisions, and conduct proper oversight, Congress must have this information. As noted above, transparency with the American people and the civilians around the world we aim to protect is essential to the long-term credibility of American counterterrorism policy and American leadership. Some Members of Congress have made requests, offered amendments, filibustered bills to acquire pieces of this information. Such a piecemeal approach will not achieve the goal of making America safer and counterterrorism activities more sustainable: Coherence and a commitment to an articulated standard of transparency will make the drone strategy more defensible and effective.

To that end, Human Rights First recommends that Congress connect its action on the AUMF, and its funding for the use of lethal force outside active zones of hostilities, to the release of the following information:

(1) A list of organizations or groups the United States considers itself to be at war with;

(2) A list of organizations or groups the United States considers to be "associated forces";

(3) The specific laws and legal interpretations each U.S. Government agency involved relies upon in its use of lethal force, within and outside of armed conflicts, including: (a) An unclassified version of the Presidential Policy Guidance referenced by President Obama in his May 23, 2013, speech at the National Defense University [22] and (b) all relevant Department of Justice legal memos;

(4) Where, when, and under what circumstances the U.S. believes it is using lethal targeting within an armed conflict, and where, when, and under what circumstances it believes it is acting outside an armed conflict;

(5) The countries where the U.S. has conducted targeted killings since September 11, 2001, and identities of all individuals killed, both in the past and going forward; how each U.S. agency involved determines who has been killed after a strike; how each agency classifies those killed as "civilian," "militant" or "combatant"; and summaries of all post-strike investigations, including who was killed, who was killed erroneously or constitutes "collateral damage" and whether and when apologies and/or compensation were provided for mistaken or collateral killings;

(6) The criteria each U.S. agency involved (read: Department of Defense and CIA) uses to decide whom it may target with lethal force—that is, who constitutes a targetable member of Al Qaeda, the Taliban, or an "associated force;" what signatures are used to justify "signature strikes"; and what exactly constitutes an "imminent threat" that justifies lethal force;

(7) An explanation of how each relevant U.S. agency decides that capture of a target is not feasible and therefore warrants the use of lethal force, and explanations going forward why capture was not feasible in each instance.

Elucidate a framework for effective post-armed conflict authorities

U.S. and international law provide a comprehensive framework within which the United States can apprehend, detain, interrogate, prosecute, and—if necessary—use lethal force against, terrorism suspects without relying on AUMF-based law of armed conflict authorities. That framework also pertains to intelligence-gathering, an issue which is not discussed here, although Washington will face the same pressures to align its espionage and surveillance activities more closely with its partners' understanding of international and domestic law, in order to retain support for its counterterrorism agenda abroad as well as at home.

Transfer, arrest, and pre-trial detention

In many cases, terrorism suspects will be arrested and prosecuted by foreign law enforcement and security officials, acting with the assistance of the United States Government and broader international community. Accordingly, building partner nation capacity to deal with threats must be the focus of a comprehensive counterterrorism strategy moving forward.

However, in some cases where the terrorism suspect is of particular interest to the United States, U.S. officials must act to effectuate the arrest, despite the fact that the suspect is located abroad and subject to foreign criminal jurisdiction.

In these cases, U.S. officials have authority to arrest terrorism suspects located abroad far before any terrorist attack has been committed or even planned. Several federal offenses apply extraterritorially, providing a basis for arresting individuals who have even limited connections to terrorist groups through providing training, money, logistical support, or other forms of assistance, irrespective of whether any terrorist attack has occurred.[23]

Terrorism suspects are often transferred to U.S. custody pursuant to extradition agreements or other formal procedures agreed upon by the U.S. and the country in which the suspect is located. In circumstances that require it, the military may effectuate capture, or assist U.S. law enforcement assets in apprehending and detaining terrorism suspects abroad.

Interrogation

While a terrorism suspect is in custody, nothing prevents government officials from interrogating that individual, and using any information secured for intelligence purposes. Some have warned that the *Miranda* requirement forces the government to tell the suspect that he may remain silent and is entitled to a lawyer, thereby compromising an ability to effectively interrogate the suspect. This is incorrect for a number of reasons.

First, in cases where there may be an ongoing terrorist threat, the public safety exception to *Miranda* would apply and government officials could interrogate the terrorism suspect and use the resulting information for any purpose, including prosecution, so long as the subject's statements are voluntary. Second, even where government agents elect to read a suspect the *Miranda* warnings, in the majority of cases the suspect waives his rights or otherwise cooperates to provide information to the agents.[24] Finally, *Miranda* violations occur, if at all, not at the point of interrogation, but only when and if the government attempts to introduce the "un-Mirandized" statements at the trial of the suspect. Therefore, government officials always retain the option of not reading a suspect the *Miranda* warnings and proceeding with an interrogation. The consequence of doing so is that government could use the information gained in such an interrogation for intelligence purposes, but not in a prosecution of the individual in question. The individual could still be prosecuted on the basis of other evidence, and even on the basis of subsequent interrogation by a "clean team" following *Miranda* warnings.[25] Intelligence gained through lawful interrogations and law enforcement interviews includes: Al Qaeda communication protocols, Al Qaeda recruiting techniques, information on Al Qaeda's finances, terrorist tradecraft used to avoid detection, information on Al Qaeda weapons programs and training, locations of Al Qaeda safe houses and training camps, information on Al Qaeda security protocols, identities of operatives involved in past and future planned attacks, and information about plots to attack U.S. targets.[26]

Prosecution

The United States retains substantial flexibility to prosecute terrorism suspects irrespective of the circumstances surrounding their initial capture and interrogation. More than 500 individuals have been prosecuted and convicted in federal courts for international terrorism-related offenses. In dozens of these cases, the defendants were initially apprehended abroad. A number of these cases involved substantial periods of pre-trial detention and interrogation, and in many cases cooperation has extended throughout the prosecution phase and into the post-conviction phase. One such case is that of Lackawanna Six defendant Yahya Goba, who pled guilty to providing material support to Al Qaeda and was sentenced to 120 months in prison, but as part of his plea agreement, continued to provide information to aid the government investigation, even testifying as a government witness in several other cases.[27]

As noted above, military commissions have been a failure in every respect; they lack global credibility and have prolonged the wait for justice for victims. Recently, 23 senior retired military leaders called the military commissions "a poor substitute for justice." [28] To the degree that an end to wartime authorities require a move away from military commissions, this will not result in the loss of an effective tool for justice but rather will prompt reliance on the more credible and effective tools of our Federal court system.

Post-conviction detention

Likewise, 13 years' experience has not indicated a necessary role for wartime authority for post-conviction detention. Hundreds of individuals convicted of terrorism-related offenses after 9/11 remain incarcerated in high-security U.S. prisons. According to Attorney General Holder, "Not one has ever escaped custody. No judicial district has suffered a retaliatory attack of any kind." [29] After serving their sentences, noncitizen U.S. terrorism suspects are subject to immediate post-conviction deportation and mandatory detention pending the conclusion of removal proceedings.

Lethal targeting

The President has said that the number of instances in which lethal targeting is the chosen tool of counterterrorism should decline. Experts and military leaders have echoed this, for both moral and practical reasons.[30] In narrow circumstances in which a terrorism suspect poses an imminent threat to the lives of Americans that cannot be dealt with through detention or other means, the President retains the authority under domestic and international law to use force against such threats. Christine Wormuth, Deputy Under Secretary of Defense, told Congress,

''The President's authority as Commander in Chief provides sufficient flexibility to respond to emerging terrorism threats posed by organizations not covered by the 2001 AUMF.'' [31] As a matter of domestic law, Article II of the Constitution provides clear authority for such operations, and Congress can and should play a role in further regulating and ensuring transparency, oversight, and accountability over such uses of force.

As a matter of international law, uses of force in self-defense against groups that committed an armed attack against the United States are permitted under Article 51 of the United Nations Charter. [32] Further, international human rights law permits using force when it is required to save lives and there is no other means to deal with a threat. [33]

The administration has made significant progress toward compliance with applicable international law in articulating through Presidential Policy Guidance (PPG) criteria governing the use of lethal force outside of active zones of hostilities. However, important questions remain. The release, with appropriate redactions, of the underlying Presidential Policy Guidance (PPG), Office of Legal Counsel (OLC) memoranda, or other information pertaining to such lethal strikes is essential for Congress to make wise decisions about how the administration is defining key terms such as ''imminence'' and ''feasibility of capture,'' whether those definitions are consistent with Article II and international law—and whether the administration is fully complying with the criteria that it has laid out. [34]

Reject proposals to expand the AUMF's mandate

The post-armed conflict framework outlined above is legally sustainable and provides operators with substantial discretion to investigate, detain, interrogate, prosecute, and—where necessary—use lethal force against terrorism suspects, irrespective of whether such individuals are connected to Al Qaeda or the 9/11 attacks. By contrast, under the current AUMF, the government is only permitted to use law of war detention to detain individuals who are determined to be part of or substantially supporting Al Qaeda, the Taliban, or an associated force in hostilities against the United States. Where the individual does not have a strong connection to core Al Qaeda, hostilities in the Afghanistan war, or the 9/11 attacks, this is a difficult legal case to make.

The weakness of the AUMF once applied beyond individuals with clear links to core Al Qaeda or 9/11 has called into question law of war detention and military commission trials at Guantanamo, as well as lethal targeting operations outside of the Afghan war theater against individuals and groups that have no connection to the 9/11 attacks.

Noting these limitations, some have argued that Congress should pass a new AUMF to provide even broader wartime authorities to use the military to detain, prosecute, and target terrorism suspects. For example, one proposal would confer onto the executive branch authority to add groups to a list that would be covered by a new AUMF, even if such groups have not attacked the United States, and are not connected to core Al Qaeda, 9/11, or the conflict in Afghanistan. [35]

Congress should reject the idea of a new or expanded AUMF for three reasons:

We have little or no evidence that preemptive U.S. military action against groups that do not pose us an imminent threat is either desired by the American people or is an operationally effective way of diminishing the long-term threat such groups do pose. Analysts have referred to groups such as Boko Haram in Nigeria, ISIS in Iraq, al-Nusra in Syria as ''emerging threats.'' There is no question that these groups are violent, anti-Western, and enormous threats to human rights and stability where they operate. But where such groups have not shown explicit capability or intention to target the security of the United States, the military activities permitted under an AUMF are the wrong response.

An expanded AUMF directed at emerging terrorist threats would pose serious legal problems without conferring clear operational benefits. An AUMF encompassing groups that have not attacked the United States, or do not pose an imminent threat of attack, would not be consistent with international law. So-called ''preemptive'' uses of force against groups and individuals are not permitted under self-defense criteria.

Similarly, authorizing AUMF-based wartime authorities in situations involving terrorist groups beyond active zones of hostilities would not be consistent with the laws of war, which can only be applied in ''armed conflict''—situations involving hostilities of sufficient intensity with organized armed groups. Although some groups, such as Boko Haram or Al Qaeda in the Islamic Maghreb, pose a serious threat in areas in which they operate, the United States is not engaged in an armed conflict with these groups under the laws of war and thus an AUMF directed at these groups would not be appropriate. [36]

An AUMF directed at emerging threats also poses serious constitutional problems. Some have noted that an AUMF conferring authority to the executive branch to use force generally against emerging terrorist threats—without clear and specific limits—would run afoul of separation of powers principles, which require Congress to clearly define the scope of the authority conferred.[37] Similarly, providing to the executive branch authority to bring new groups within an AUMF could constitute a violation of the nondelegation doctrine because Congress would be unconstitutionally delegating authority that is committed by the Constitution to the legislative branch.

Finally, *the value of an AUMF must be weighed against the risk of its use as a future blank check.* The drafters of the 2001 AUMF have stressed that it is being used in ways they did not intend.[38] Nothing would prevent this or a future administration from using even a carefully crafted new AUMF to justify another large-scale invasion or costly war without further congressional debate or authorization.

SITUATIONS IN WHICH A NEW AUMF MAY BE APPROPRIATE

As noted, it is highly problematic as a matter of law and policy to expand the existing AUMF or pass a new one to target emerging terrorist threats that have not attacked the United States and do not pose an imminent threat of attack. Further, the United States has the authority under domestic and international law to use force to deal with imminent threats absent an AUMF. For these reasons, the administration has not requested additional AUMF authority and the President has indicated that he will not sign legislation that expands the AUMF's mandate.[39]

However, there are circumstances in which an AUMF would be an appropriate and lawful response to a threat. The clearest example would be if the United States was attacked on a large-scale and Congress and the President intended to engage in a prolonged and sustained military campaign, which rose to the level of armed conflict, against one or more responsible armed groups. History also provides examples of Presidents choosing to act under imminent threat, and then come to Congress for authorization for an extended engagement. Congress has proven itself able to move quickly and supportively in such instances, and there is no reason to believe that has changed.

In addition, in some situations, the United States may choose to engage on a prolonged basis in an ongoing armed conflict even if the United States has not yet been attacked. For example, if the United States were to decide to engage in military attacks on a sustained basis in the ongoing armed conflict in Syria, it would be appropriate for the executive branch to secure an AUMF from Congress before doing so. Similarly, most experts agree that there is an ongoing armed conflict in Yemen, and though Human Rights First does not take a position on whether that conflict is wise, the Congress may choose to authorize the United States to engage alongside the Yemeni Government in that armed conflict.

CONCLUSION

The work of protecting the United States from terrorist violence is far from done. Yet it is increasingly clear that, both for effective counterterrorism and for preserving U.S. stature as a leader on human rights and the rule of law, the 2001 AUMF and the wartime attitudes and policies it has facilitated are outdated. The domestic and international laws that built a strong wall between wartime and peacetime have a vital policy purpose; absent them, powers that were once extraordinary become the norm, and policies that are the hallmarks of dictatorships become associated with America. Congress and the administration have the opportunity to move beyond piecemeal attempts at reform to set a clear legal and policy framework that combats terrorism effectively and makes clear to our friends and enemies that we will not be goaded into eroding our national strength through a permanent state of war. Human Rights First supports this goal and looks forward to engaging in the hard work of elaborating specific legal and policy understandings on these vital questions.

End Notes

[1] Authorization for Use of Military Force § 2(a), 115 Stat. 224, 224 (codified at 50 U.S.C. § 1541 note) (2001).

[2] *Hamdi* v. *Rumsfeld*, 542 U.S. 507, 521 (2004).

[3] Karen DeYoung, ''Afghan War's Approaching End Throws Legal Status of Guantanamo Detainees into Doubt,'' Wash. Post, Oct. 18, 2013.

[4] Hon. Jeh Charles Johnson, General Counsel, U.S. Dep't of Def., ''The Conflict Against Al Qaeda and its Affiliates: How Will It End?,'' Speech Before the Oxford Union (Nov. 30, 2012).

[5] Linda J. Bilmes, "The Financial Legacy of Iraq and Afghanistan: How Wartime Spending Decisions Will Constrain Future National Security Budgets" (Cambridge, MA: Harvard Kennedy School, 2013), p. 3.

[6] Ann Scott Tyson, "Heavy Troop Deployments Are Called Major Risk," The Washington Post (Washington, DC, United States), April 2, 2008.

[7] George F. Kennan ("X"), "The Sources of Soviet Conduct," Foreign Aff., July 1947.

[8] Pew has documented a marked decrease in global approval of the administration's international policy including drone strikes. See, e.g., "Global Opinion of Obama Slips, International Policies Faulted: Drone Strikes Widely Opposed," Pew Res. Global Attitudes Project (June 13, 2012).

[9] Jo Becker & Scott Shane, "Secret 'Kill List' Proves a Test of Obama's Principles and Will," N.Y. Times, May 29, 2012, at A1.

[10] Holger Stark, "Drone Killing Debate: Germany Limits Information Exchange with US Intelligence," Spiegel Online Int'l (May 17, 2011).

[11] Eric Holder, Att'y Gen., Address at Northwestern University Law School (March 5, 2012).

[12] White House Plan for Closing the Guantanamo Bay Detention Facility (July 24, 2013).

[13] John O. Brennan, Assistant to the President for Homeland Sec. and Counterterrorism, Remarks at Woodrow Wilson Int'l Ctr. for Scholars: The Ethics and Efficacy of the President's Counterterrorism Strategy (Apr. 30, 2012).

[14] Kimberly Dozier, "Exclusive: CIA Falls Back in Afghanistan," The Daily Beast (May 4, 2014).

[15] Adam Serwer, "Courts Can Win Terror Convictions After All," MSNBC (March 26, 2014).

[16] President Barack Obama, Remarks by the President at the Nat'l Def. Univ. (May 23, 2013) [hereinafter NDU Speech].

[17] Kate Brannen, "Leon Panetta: Al Qaeda's Leadership 'Decimated'", Politico (Nov. 21, 2012).

[18] "Al-Nusra Commits to Al Qaeda, Deny Iraq Branch 'Merger'", Naharnet (April 10, 2013).

[19] Michael Stothard, William Wallis & Javier Blas, "West African Nations Pledge United Front against Boko Haram," Fin. Times, (May 19, 2014).

[20] Abu Bakr Al-Baghdadi, head of ISIS, scoffed that "I have to choose between the rule of God and the rule of Al Zawahiri, and I choose the rule of God. See, e.g. Aryn Baker, "Why Al-Qaeda Kicked out its Deadly Syria Franchise," Time (Feb. 3, 2014).

[21] NDU Speech, supra note 16.

[22] NDU Speech, supra note 16.

[23] See generally Charles Doyle, Cong. Research Serv., 94–166, Extraterritorial Application of American Criminal Law (2012).

[24] Richard B. Zabel & James J. Benjamin, Jr., in Pursuit of Justice: 2009 Update and Recent Developments 30, Human Rights First (2009).

[25] See, e.g., Benjamin Weiser, "Hearing on Terror Suspect Explores Miranda Warning," N.Y. Times, Dec. 13, 2011, at A31.

[26] See generally David S. Kris, "Law Enforcement as a Counterterrorism Tool," 5 J. Nat'l. Security L. & Pol'y 1 (2011).

[27] Richard B. Zabel & James J. Benjamin, Jr., In Pursuit of Justice: Prosecuting Terrorism Cases in Federal Courts 118–19, Human Rights First (2008).

[28] Letter from retired U.S. generals and admirals to Senators Richard Durbin and Ted Cruz, Chairman and Ranking Member, Senate Judiciary Committee, Re: Subcommittee on the Constitution, Civil Rights and Human Rights Hearing on Closing Guantanamo: The National Security, Fiscal, and Human Rights Implications (July 24, 2013).

[29] Eric Holder, Att'y Gen., Address at the Univ. of Cal. Berkeley School of Law Commencement (May 11, 2013).

[30] See generally Joshua Foust, Oversight for Effectiveness: A Counterterrorism Perspective on the Targeted Killings "White Paper," Nat'l Sec. Network (2013).

[31] Advance Questions for Christine E. Wormuth, Nominee for the Position of Under Secretary of Defense for Policy, S. Armed Serv. Comm. (Feb. 25, 2014).

[32] U.N. Charter art. 51.

[33] Report of the Special Rapporteur on extrajudicial, summary, or arbitrary executions, Philip Alston, U.N. Doc. A/HRC/14/24/Add.6 (May 28, 2010).

[34] In active zones of hostilities where the United States may be using force to aid a foreign government in an armed conflict against a local group with terrorism-related ties, broader law-of-war based lethal targeting authorities would continue to apply.

[35] Robert Chesney, Jack Goldsmith, Matthew C. Waxman, & Benjamin Wittes, A Statutory Framework for Next—Generation Terrorist Threats, Hoover Inst. (2013).

[36] Although an AUMF does not constitute a Declaration of War under domestic law and cannot create a state of armed conflict under international law, historically AUMFs have nonetheless constituted, in effect, war authorizations and signaled an intent to engage in armed conflict.

[37] Jennifer Daskal & Steve Vladeck, After the AUMF: "A Response to Chesney, Goldsmith, Waxman, and Wittes," Lawfare (March 17, 2013).

[38] See Andrew Rosenthal, Op-Ed., "The Forever War," N.Y. Times Taking Note (May 17, 2013); Jack Goldsmith, "Congress Must Figure Out What Our Government Is Doing In the Name of the AUMF," Lawfare (May 17, 2013).

[39] NDU Speech, supra note 16.

RESPONSES OF STEPHEN W. PRESTON TO QUESTIONS
SUBMITTED BY SENATOR BOB CORKER

Question. Imminent Threats.—In answering the below question, please in every instance clearly distinguish between which portions of your answers relate to: legal

72

authorities versus policy guidance; U.S. versus international law; and the authorities granted by the 9/11 AUMF versus those granted by Article II of the Constitution.

In your testimony, you discussed the authority of the President to use lethal force against ''imminent'' threats to the United States.

♦ Please define ''imminent'' and explain in detail both the legal authorities on which that definition is based and how the administration arrived at that defi- nition. Does a group that has previously conducted an attack against Americans constitute an imminent threat?

Answer. Article II of the Constitution provides the President with the authority to take military action for the purpose of protecting important national interests, and stopping an imminent threat would be a clear and compelling example of an important national interest. Clearly, an individual or group that is planning a specific attack to take place in the near term and that has the capability to carry out such plans would constitute an imminent threat. Attorney General Holder, in his remarks on March 5, 2012, at Northwestern University School of Law, explained that the determination of whether an individual presents an ''imminent'' threat may incorporate consideration of (1) the relevant window of opportunity to act against that individual, (2) the possible harm that missing the window would cause to civilians, and (3) the likelihood of heading off future disastrous attacks against the United States. As the Attorney General said:

As we learned on 9/11, al-Qaeda has demonstrated the ability to strike with little or no notice—and to cause devastating casualties. Its leaders are continually planning attacks against the United States, and they do not behave like a traditional military—wearing uniforms, carrying arms openly, or massing forces in preparation for an attack. Given these facts, the Constitution does not require the President to delay action until some theoretical end-stage of planning—when the precise time, place, and manner of an attack become clear. Such a requirement would create an unacceptably high risk that our efforts would fail, and that Americans would be killed.

Indeed, in comments similar to the Attorney General's, John Brennan, then-Assistant to the President for Homeland Security and Counterterrorism, noted in his speech at Harvard Law School in September 2011 that we are finding increasing recognition in the international community that a more flexible understanding of ''imminence'' may be appropriate when dealing with terrorist groups and that what constitutes an ''imminent'' attack should be broadened in light of the modern-day capabilities, techniques, and technological innovations of terrorist organizations. Timely, credible, and accurate intelligence and information are critical in determining whether an individual or group presents a ''continuing, imminent threat to U.S. persons.''

Question. Lethal Action Against al-Qaeda.—In answering the below question, please in every instance clearly distinguish between which portions of your answers relate to: legal authorities versus policy guidance; U.S. versus international law; and the authorities granted by the 9/11 AUMF versus those granted by Article II of the Constitution.

♦ Does the 9/11 AUMF authorize the President to take lethal action against al-Qaeda or its members or its associated forces regardless of whether they pose an imminent threat? Does the United States currently undertake lethal action outside of Afghanistan against al-Qaeda or its members or its associated forces where they do not pose an imminent threat?

Answer. The AUMF authorizes the use of military force against al-Qaeda, the Taliban, and associated forces. This authority is not limited to imminent threats.

Pursuant to the President's policy guidance, the Department of Defense currently undertakes lethal counterterrorism direct action outside the United States and areas of active hostilities only against targets that pose a continuing, imminent threat to U.S. persons.

Question. Lethal Action Against Nonimminent Threats.—In answering the below question, please in every instance clearly distinguish between which portions of your answers relate to: legal authorities versus policy guidance; U.S. versus international law; and the authorities granted by the 9/11 AUMF versus those granted by Article II of the Constitution.

♦ Does the 9/11 AUMF authorize the President to take lethal action against foreign individuals or members of foreign terrorist organizations (other than al-Qaeda or its members or its associated forces) that do not pose an imminent threat?

Answer. The AUMF authorizes the use of military force against al-Qaeda, the Taliban, and associated forces. This authority does not depend on whether there is an imminent threat.

Question. Article II Lethal Action Authorities.—In answering the below question, please in every instance clearly distinguish between which portions of your answers relate to: legal authorities versus policy guidance; U.S. versus international law; and the authorities granted by the 9/11 AUMF versus those granted by Article II of the Constitution.

◆ Does Article II authorize the President to take lethal action against foreign individuals or members of foreign terrorist organizations that do not pose an imminent threat?

Answer. Article II of the Constitution provides the President with the authority to take military action for the purpose of protecting important national interests. Any use of military force by the United States would be governed by the law of armed conflict, which includes limitations on the use of military force to actions that are necessary and proportionate and that are consistent with the principles of distinction and proportionality.

Pursuant to the President's policy guidance, the Department of Defense currently undertakes lethal counterterrorism direct action outside the United States and areas of active hostilities only against targets that pose a continuing, imminent threat to U.S. persons.

Question. Lethal Action Taken.—Has the administration taken lethal action against members of a foreign terrorist organization that was not covered by the 9/11 AUMF?

Answer. Yes. For example, members of the designated foreign terrorist organization Kata'ib Hezbollah were reportedly among those killed in the course of U.S. or combined U.S.-Iraq military operations in Iraq during Operation IRAQI FREEDOM.

Question. Extent of AUMF Authorities.—In answering the below question, please in every instance clearly distinguish between which portions of your answers relate to: legal authorities versus policy guidance; U.S. versus international law; and the authorities granted by the 9/11 AUMF versus those granted by Article II of the Constitution.

◆ Does the AUMF authorize the President to use force against groups or individuals that pose a threat, imminent or otherwise, to anyone or anything other than the United States and U.S. persons? What about U.S. coalition partners whether located inside or outside Afghanistan? What about U.S. allies? What about U.S. national security or other U.S. national interests?

Answer. The 2001 AUMF authorizes the President to use military force against al-Qaeda, the Taliban, and associated forces. As those groups also present ongoing threats to a number of U.S. coalition partners and allies, U.S. counterterrorism operations pursuant to the 2001 AUMF serve mutual interests of the United States and those partners and allies.

Question. Article II Versus AUMF.—In answering the below question, please in every instance clearly distinguish between which portions of your answers relate to: legal authorities versus policy guidance; U.S. versus international law; and the authorities granted by the 9/11 AUMF versus those granted by Article II of the Constitution.

◆ If the AUMF is repealed, how does the scope of Article II authority differ, if at all, from current U.S. policy governing the use of force outside of Afghanistan?

Answer. The AUMF authorizes the use of military force against al-Qaeda, the Taliban, and associated forces. This authority does not depend on whether any such group poses a threat of imminent attack. Article II of the Constitution provides the President with the authority to take military action for the purpose of protecting important national interests. Pursuant to the President's policy guidance, the Department of Defense currently undertakes lethal counterterrorism direct action outside the United States and areas of active hostilities only against targets that pose a continuing, imminent threat to U.S. persons regardless of the legal authority for that action.

Question. Presidential Guidance.—Will you provide the Senate Foreign Relations Committee with the text of any current or prior Presidential policy guidance related to the 9/11 AUMF?

Answer. The administration is committed to keeping the appropriate congressional committees fully informed of matters within their jurisdiction, and consistent with this commitment, senior administration officials have briefed the Congress on the written policy standards and procedures approved by the President in May 2013, concerning operations to capture or employ lethal force against terrorist targets outside the United States and outside areas of active hostilities. Beyond that, access to Presidential policy guidance related to the 9/11 AUMF is not controlled by the Department of Defense. I have therefore referred your request for the text of any such Presidential guidance to the White House.

Question. Exceptions to Policy.—Does the Presidential policy guidance related to the 9/11 AUMF provide for exceptions to its baseline policy requirements, and, if so, have such exceptions been employed and in what circumstances? Has the administration ever failed to apply, or has it ever deviated from, any applicable Presidential policy guidance related to the 9/11 AUMF in the use of lethal force?

Answer. As noted in the section captioned ''Reservation of Authority'' of the May 2013 fact sheet on U.S. Policy Standards and Procedures for the Use of Force in Counterterrorism Operations Outside the United States and Areas of Active Hostilities, those standards and procedures do not limit the President's authority to take action in extraordinary circumstances when doing so is both lawful and necessary to protect the United States or its allies. To date, the President has not authorized any Department of Defense counterterrorism operations under this ''extraordinary circumstances'' exception to the policy standards.

Question. Feasibility of Capture.—The administration has limited lethal action to those individuals ''whose capture is not feasible.'' How is the feasibility of capture determined? What factors are considered and how are they balanced? Is the feasibility determination made with or without consideration of factors relating to the use of lethal force? In other words, is the feasibility, or comparative advantage, of the use of lethal force a factor in determining the feasibility of capture in that instance?

Answer. There is no rigid formula for evaluating feasibility of capture; it is a judgment based on the facts and circumstances in the particular situation. Military determinations about feasibility of capture are largely driven by an assessment of risks, such as the risk to the capturing forces, the risk of civilian casualties, and the risk that the operation may not be successful.

Question. New Terrorist Groups.—Have any foreign terrorist groups been covered by, or targeted under, the AUMF, at any time since its enactment, that were not in existence on 9/11/2001? If so, how many?

Answer. Yes. For example, as I noted in my prepared remarks, in Afghanistan, the U.S. military currently conducts operations pursuant to the AUMF against al-Qaeda, the Taliban, and other terrorist and insurgent groups that are engaged alongside al-Qaeda and the Taliban in hostilities against the United States or its coalition partners. In addition, the International Security Assistance Force and U.S. rules of engagement permit targeting of hostile personnel in Afghanistan based on the threat they pose to U.S., coalition, and Afghan forces or to civilians.

To give another example, as I noted in my prepared remarks, in Yemen, the U.S. military has conducted direct action under the 2001 AUMF targeting members of Al Qaeda in the Arabian Peninsula (AQAP), which is an organized, armed group that is part of, or at least an associated force of, al-Qaeda. AQAP was not known by its current name until 2007, but al-Qaeda has been present in Yemen in some form since before the attacks of September 11, 2001. Al-Qaeda was responsible for the attack on the USS *COLE* in Yemen in October 2000.

Question. List of Terrorist Organizations.—Does the administration maintain a list of terrorist organizations that fall within the 9/11 AUMF? If so, can this list be shared with the Foreign Relations Committee either in a public or classified setting?

Answer. In my prepared remarks, I described the three contexts in which the United States is currently relying on the 2001 AUMF and the groups against which the U.S. military has taken direct action pursuant to the AUMF.

Beyond those groups against which we have taken or contemplated taking military action, we do not maintain a comprehensive list of all groups that theoretically could be subject to military action pursuant to the AUMF. Whether any particular group is an ''associated force'' of al-Qaeda is a fact-intensive inquiry that requires a careful examination of relevant intelligence at the time military action is being contemplated. The administration generally undertakes that careful examination only if a concrete situation is presented for review. Accordingly, the fact that a terrorist group has not been determined to be an associated force of al-Qaeda does not mean that the administration has made a final determination that the group is not an associated force.

Per your request during the hearing, additional information on this topic has been provided by separate, classified communication to the committee.

Question. Definition of Associated Force.—How do you define the term "associated force" with respect to al-Qaeda and the Taliban? What factors are considered in making the "associated force" determination? What level of confidence is required, and what legal standard must be met, in making such a determination? Would any of the following be sufficient on its own for a group to constitute an "associated force" of al-Qaeda: (1) a group's pledge of loyalty to al-Qaeda; (2) adoption of the al-Qaeda brand; (3) acceptance of al-Qaeda's command and control; (4) adherence to al-Qaeda's ideology; and (5) use of al-Qaeda's tactics, techniques, and procedures. What if in addition there is intelligence indicating that members of the group are actively planning operations against U.S. persons? Would a group's explicit rejection of affiliation with al-Qaeda and of its command and control be sufficient to remove such a group from coverage by the 9/11 AUMF? What if in addition there is intelligence indicating that members of the group share al-Qaeda's goal of targeting U.S. persons? What if in addition there is intelligence indicating that members of the group are actively planning operations against U.S. persons?

Answer. As I indicated in my prepared remarks, the concept of an "associated force" is based on the well-established concept of cobelligerency in the law of war. To be an "associated force" of al-Qaeda or the Taliban, a group must be both (1) an organized, armed group that has entered the fight alongside al-Qaeda or the Taliban and (2) a cobelligerent with al-Qaeda or the Taliban in hostilities against the United States or its coalition partners. A group that embraces al-Qaeda's ideology without actually joining the fight alongside al-Qaeda is not an "associated force," nor is every group that commits or threatens to commit terrorist acts against U.S. persons an "associated force."

Question. AUMF and the Taliban Post-2014.—Does it continue to be the policy of the President that all combat operations in Afghanistan by U.S. Armed Forces will end in 2014? If so, will the 9/11 AUMF continue to apply to the Taliban after January 2015? If not, is it possible that United States will nevertheless remain in a state of armed conflict with the Taliban for purposes of international law?

Answer. As described in the President's May 27, 2014, speech as well as his most recent State of the Union Address, if the Afghan Government signs a security agreement that we have negotiated, a small force of Americans could remain in Afghanistan with NATO allies to carry out two narrow missions: training and assisting Afghan forces, and counterterrorism operations to pursue any remnants of al-Qaeda. The President has been clear that it is not in our interest to remain on a perpetual wartime footing, and that this war, like all others, must at some point come to an end.

The change in the U.S. military mission in Afghanistan is an important milestone, but it will not in itself mean that the 2001 AUMF will not apply to the Taliban after 2014. Whether and to what extent an armed conflict with the Taliban continues will need to be assessed at that time based on conditions on the ground.

Question. Law of War Detention Against Taliban.—Will the President maintain the ability to conduct law of war detention against members of the Taliban and its associated forces after January 2015?

Answer. The change in the U.S. military mission in Afghanistan is an important milestone, but it will not in itself mean that the United States will no longer have authority to detain members of the Taliban in law of war detention after 2014. Whether, and to what extent, an armed conflict with the Taliban continues will need to be assessed at that time based on conditions in Afghanistan.

Question. Termination of Active Military Operations in Afghanistan.—Are there any legal implications of the termination of active military operations in Afghanistan on the ability of the United States to conduct lethal or detention operations under the 9/11 AUMF against al-Qaeda and its associated forces? Are detention authorities under the 9/11 AUMF against al-Qaeda and its associated forces dependent on the existence of a "hot battlefield"? What locations are considered today by the administration to be a "hot battlefield"?

Answer. The change in the U.S. military mission in Afghanistan is an important milestone, but it will not in itself mean that the 2001 AUMF will not apply to al-Qaeda and associated forces after 2014. The United States will continue to have legal authority to detain individuals from the al-Qaeda, and associated forces until the end of the armed conflict, as a matter of international law, and under the

AUMF. As Ms. McLeod noted in her prepared remarks, we remain optimistic that there will come a point when our efforts to disrupt, dismantle, and defeat al-Qaeda have succeeded to such an extent that we will no longer describe ourselves as being in an ''armed conflict'' with al-Qaeda to which the law of war applies.

Question. Presidential Action Regarding AUMF.—Can the authorities provided by the 9/11 AUMF be terminated by the President acting alone, including through a statement declaring the end of the conflict? Can the President terminate the 9/11 AUMF in part (i.e., terminate with respect to a specific group but not to others)? If so, by what mechanism?

Answer. The President has expressed his commitment to move the United States off a permanent war footing and has made clear the intent to engage with Congress to ''refine, and ultimately repeal'' the AUMF. The President cannot, acting alone, repeal the AUMF, which is a U.S. statute. However, military operations that the AUMF authorizes are, like all U.S. military operations, subject to the President's direction and control. Thus, the President could issue guidance limiting the military operations conducted pursuant to the AUMF. Additionally, a cessation of hostilities between the United States and al-Qaeda or the Taliban could mark the end of the armed conflict, after which the use of U.S. military force in the prosecution of that conflict would no longer be necessary and might be inconsistent with international law.

Question. AUMF Termination.—Would the termination of the 9/11 AUMF toward any or all covered groups, whether by congressional action to repeal or by the President acting alone, end the armed conflict with such groups under international law, including with al-Qaeda?

Answer. The repeal of the AUMF would not, in itself, necessarily end the conflict between the United States and al-Qaeda or the Taliban under international law. Whether and to what extent an armed conflict with the Taliban continued at that point would need to be assessed at that time based on conditions on the ground.

Question. End of Armed Conflict Terminating AUMF.—Would the end of the ''armed conflict'' for purposes of international law with all groups covered by the 9/11 AUMF terminate the authorities granted to the President by the 9/11 AUMF?

Answer. The end of the armed conflict between the United States and al-Qaeda and the Taliban would not itself terminate the 2001 AUMF. The AUMF is a U.S. statute that can only be modified or rescinded through the process prescribed in the U.S. Constitution.

Question. Article II Authority for Detention.—In your testimony, you discussed the Article II authority of the President to use lethal force against an imminent and continuing threat to the United States. In such an instance, and in the absence of statutory authorization, would the President also have an Article II authority to detain enemy combatants under the laws of war? If so, what are the legal parameters of such a detention authority, including at what point would such a detention authority terminate? Is such a detention authority coextensive with the detention authority currently provided by the 9/11 AUMF as it relates to al-Qaeda and its associated forces? If not, does that factor weigh in favor of the use of lethal force in any way, including when assessing the ''feasibility of capture''?

Answer. Where the President has authority under Article II to use lethal force against individuals who pose an imminent terrorist threat to the United States, he would also have authority to detain individuals posing that threat for some period of time. The legal parameters of the President's authority for military detention in the absence of a statutory authorization are an unsettled area of law, (in part because military detention in the current conflict has been pursuant to the 2001 AUMF). That said, any legal uncertainty about the long-term disposition of captured terrorists would not be a factor relevant to the ''feasibility of capture.'' It is the President's policy that capture is preferred whenever feasible.

Question. Article II Authority for Use of Lethal Force Versus Detention.—Are there circumstances where the President has Article II authority to use lethal force, but where he lacks law of war detention authority? In such a circumstance, would the lack of detention authority be a factor weighing in favor of the use of lethal force in any way, including when assessing the ''feasibility of capture''?

Answer. The answer to both questions is ''No.'' Where the President has authority under Article II of the Constitution to employ lethal military force against individuals who pose a continuing imminent terrorist threat to the United States, he would also have authority to detain individuals posing that threat for some period of time. The legal parameters of the President's authority for military detention in the absence of a statutory authorization are an unsettled area of law (in part because military detention in the current conflict has been pursuant to the 2001 AUMF). Any legal uncertainty regarding the long-term disposition of a detainee would not be a factor in applying the President's policy preference to capture rather than kill terrorist suspects when capture is feasible.

RESPONSES OF MARY MCLEOD TO QUESTIONS
SUBMITTED BY SENATOR BOB CORKER

Question. In answering the below questions, please in every instance clearly distinguish between which portions of your answers that relate to: legal authorities versus policy guidance; U.S. versus international law; and the authorities granted by the 9/11 AUMF versus those granted by Article II of the Constitution.

◆ Does the April 1, 2011, OLC Memorandum on Authority to Use Military Force in Libya reflect the administration's current understanding of Presidential authority to take military action without prior congressional authorization?

Answer. Yes, the April 1, 2011, OLC Memorandum on Authority to Use Military Force in Libya continues to reflect the administration's position on the scope of Presidential authority to take military action without prior congressional authorization for the operations under consideration in that Memorandum.

Question. The Libya OLC Memo states: "We have acknowledged *one possible constitutionally based limit* on [. . .] Presidential authority to employ military force in defense of important national interests—a *planned* military engagement that constitutes a *'war'* within the meaning of the Declaration of War Clause *may* require prior congressional authorization"(emphasis added).

◆ Does this administration believe that conflict that constitutes a "war" within the meaning of the Declaration of War Clause might not require prior congressional authorization?
◆ If so, under what circumstances?
◆ Was congressional authorization necessary under the Constitution to conduct Operation Iraqi Freedom?
◆ Was congressional authorization required at any point under the War Powers Resolution to conduct Operation Iraqi Freedom? If so at what point?
◆ What is the definition of a "planned" military operation?

Answer. While acknowledging a possible constitutionally based limitation on Presidential authority under the Constitution to employ military force in cases involving a planned military operation that constitutes a war within the meaning of the Declaration of War clause, the OLC Memorandum in question concluded that the anticipated nature, scope, and duration of the operations under consideration did not rise to the level of war in the sense of that clause. At the same time, this and other OLC opinions have recognized the congressional interest, including as reflected in the War Powers Resolution, in providing express congressional authorization for the use of force by the U.S. military in major, prolonged conflicts such as the wars in Vietnam and Korea, where a fact-specific assessment has been conducted regarding the anticipated nature, scope, and duration of the planned military operations and of the exposure of U.S. military personnel to significant risk over a substantial period. By providing for United States involvement in hostilities to continue for 60 days (or 90 days for military necessity), Congress signaled in the War Powers Resolution that it considers express congressional authorization most critical for such major, prolonged conflicts.

While what constitutes a "planned" military operation is a fact-specific question, the President decided to seek an Authorization to Use Military Force for Iraq in 2002 prior to the commencement of Operation Iraqi Freedom, the Congress provided such an authorization in H.J. Res. 114, and the President in his signing statement set forth his position in relation to that authorization. These actions by Congress and the President moot the question whether such an authorization would have been required under the Constitution and the War Powers Resolution. Given international concerns with Iraq's weapons of mass destruction (WMD) program and Iraq's failure to comply with relevant United Nations Security Council resolutions, there was a sustained period of almost 10 months of preparation and planning for possible military action while the United States and others sought a diplomatic resolution of the crisis. In addition to publicly signaling the ongoing planning for military operations by passing the AUMF-Iraq, the United States actively sought (and received) commitments from a number of allies and partners for the deployment of a multinational force in the event that it became necessary to enforce applicable United Nations Security Council resolutions through military force.

Question. According to the Libya OLC memo, the President has the constitutional authority to use force if he can "reasonably determine that such use of force [is] in the national interest."

◆ Can the President take lethal action against foreign individuals or members of foreign terrorist organizations that do not pose an imminent threat so long as he determines it is in the national interest to do so?

◆ If so, what if any limits are there on such action?

Answer. As the April 1, 2011, OLC memorandum indicated, the President has authority under the Constitution to use force not amounting to "war" in the constitutional sense, where he reasonably determines that such force is in the national interest, at least insofar as the Congress has not specifically restricted it by statute. In the case of Libya, the OLC memorandum identified regional stability and supporting the U.N. Security Council's credibility and effectiveness as a sufficient basis to justify, under Article II of the Constitution, the President's use of military force in Libya (a determination that did not involve a conclusion that Libya or any Libyan party posed an imminent threat to the United States). Whether and how the President's constitutional authority to use force might be invoked in future cases, including the determination of the national interests that form the basis of potential military actions, will necessarily turn on the particular facts of those cases.

As indicated in my testimony, any use of military force by the United States would be governed by international law. Under international law, the United States has an inherent right of self-defense to use force to respond to an armed attack, or the imminent threat of an armed attack. In addition, the United States may use military force on the basis of State consent or when authorized to do so by the UN Security Council. In the case of Libya, on March 28, 2011, the UN Security Council adopted Resolution 1973, which authorized member states, acting individually or through regional organizations, "to take all necessary measures . . . to protect civilians and civilian populated areas under threat of attack" in Libya.

Question. Can a conflict constitute a "war" within the meaning of the Declaration of War Clause, or constitute "hostilities" for the purposes of the War Powers Resolution, in situations where the U.S. takes military action but there are no "boots on the ground"?

At what point or under what circumstances do unmanned drone strikes constitute a "war" within the meaning of the Declaration of War Clause, or constitute "hostilities" for the purposes of the War Powers Resolution?

Answer. Whether the use of military force constitutes a "war" within the meaning of the Declaration of War Clause would, as described in previous OLC opinions, involve the need for a fact-specific assessment of the anticipated nature, scope, and duration of the planned military operations and of the exposure of U.S. military personnel to significant risk over a substantial period. Whether a military operation rises to level of "hostilities" for purposes of the War Powers Resolution similarly is a fact-based assessment. Whether there are "boots on the ground," and how and to what extent the United States may be employing unmanned aerial vehicles or other weapons systems, would be among the considerations in conducting such assessments, but it is not possible in the absence of a specific factual context to anticipate how those factors would be assessed in every case.

Question. In your testimony, you appeared to suggest the President had the authority to strike Syria after the August 2013 chemical weapons attack without congressional authorization. Is this the position of the administration?

◆ If so, under what specific constitutional and statutory authority would those strikes have been conducted?

◆ Please also provide your analysis of how such authorities apply to permit such strikes.

◆ Under what theory of international law would such strikes be authorized?

◆ Would the President have been required to notify Congress or seek congressional authorization pursuant to the War Powers Resolution of any such strikes?

Answer. In his August 31, 2013, Rose Garden speech, the President communicated his decision to seek authorization for the use of force from the American people's representatives in Congress prior to taking military action against targets in Syria. In describing the planned military action, he explained that U.S. military action in Syria would not be an open-ended intervention and would not involve putting "boots on the ground," and that instead military action would be designed to be limited in duration and scope. In explaining his decision, the President said that "while I believe I have the authority to carry out this military action without specific congressional authorization, I know that the country will be stronger if we take this course, and our actions will be even more effective." As the crisis was avoided and no military engagement in fact occurred, it is not possible to assess the precise nature and scope of notifications and reports that would have been provided consistent with the War Powers Resolution had military action taken place.

The administration did not present a position on the international law implications of a possible Syrian military engagement in August 2013, although the President made clear in his August 31, 2013, speech that he was prepared to take military action "without the approval of a United Nations Security Council that, so far, has been completely paralyzed and unwilling to hold Assad accountable." Any finalized U.S. position on this question would have been articulated after close consultation with allies as part of our efforts to develop a coalition to pursue military action; the resolution of the crisis through Syria's agreement to disarm its chemical weapons capabilities in accordance with United Nations Security Council Resolution 2118 obviated the need for these consultations.

———

RESPONSES OF STEPHEN W. PRESTON TO QUESTIONS
SUBMITTED BY SENATOR BENJAMIN L. CARDIN

DOD DIRECTIVE 2311.01E REPORTABLE INCIDENTS

Department of Defense Directive Number 2311.01E requires that "all reportable incidents committed by, or against, U.S. personnel" be "investigated thoroughly, and where appropriate, remedied by corrective action." This reflects law of war and international human rights law requirements to investigate potentially unlawful killings.

Question. What steps are U.S .personnel required to take to investigate reports of civilian deaths or potentially unlawful deaths, including from drone strikes, as a matter of law and U.S. policy?

Answer. The United States goes to great lengths to avoid civilian casualties, providing protections as a matter of policy that go well beyond those required by the law of armed conflict. Unfortunately, civilian injuries or deaths may occur in U.S. counterterrorism operations despite these precautions. Where there is credible information that civilians may have been injured or killed, the United States investigates the matter, drawing on available information to make an informed determination about whether civilians were, in fact, injured or killed. After-action reviews are conducted both to ascertain what occurred and to ensure that the United States is taking the most effective steps to minimize the risk of noncombatants being injured or killed in future operations. Additionally, longstanding DOD policy requires prompt reporting, thorough investigation and, where appropriate, corrective action in response to any possible, suspected, or alleged violation of the law of war for which there is credible information.

Question. Does this directive apply to all Department of Defense personnel, including those operating under Title 50 covert action authority?

Answer. DOD personnel are required to conduct themselves consistent with law of armed conflict principles at all times, and always remain subject to the War Crimes Act of 1996 and, in the case of military members, to the Uniform Code of Military Justice. DOD's long-standing practice is entirely consistent with the classified annex to the joint explanatory statement accompanying the National Defense Authorization Act for Fiscal Year 2014.

Question. How does the executive branch interpret the laws of war with regard to the authority to use lethal force and the legal definition of armed conflict?

Answer. During an armed conflict, the United States views the law of armed conflict as the relevant legal framework governing the conduct of hostilities. Under the law of armed conflict, military operations, including the use of lethal force, must comply with the principles of necessity, proportionality, distinction, and humanity. The use of force, including lethal military force, in prosecuting the armed conflict against al-Qaeda, the Taliban, and associated forces is consistent with the law of war. All U.S. military operations against al-Qaeda, the Taliban, and associated forces are conducted in a manner consistent with Common Article 3 of the Geneva Conventions and all other international law applicable in noninternational armed conflicts.

Question. In particular, how does the administration's claim to be in a global armed conflict of indefinite duration comply with the requirement for armed conflict that hostilities be between the United States and a group that is sufficiently organized and reach a level of intensity that is distinct from sporadic acts of violence?

Answer. The U.S. conflict against al-Qaeda qualifies under international law as an armed conflict not of an international character. The U.S. Supreme Court adopted this characterization in 2006 in determining that Common Article 3 of the Geneva Conventions of 1949 is applicable to detainees captured in the conflict.

RESPONSE OF MARY MCLEOD TO QUESTION
SUBMITTED BY SENATOR BENJAMIN L. CARDIN

Question. The executive branch has stated that the AUMF authorizes the use of force against al-Qaeda and its "associated forces," defined as organized armed groups that have "entered the fight alongside al-Qaeda" and are "co-belligerent[s] with al-Qaeda in hostilities against the United States or its coalition partners."

◆ What specific organizational features or conduct would lead a group to be classified as an associated force?

Answer. As indicated in previous U.S. Government statements, including in the prepared remarks for this hearing of my colleague, Stephen Preston, the concept of an "associated force" is based on the well-established concept of co-belligerency in the laws of war. To be an "associated force" of al-Qaeda or the Taliban a group must be both (1) an organized, armed group that has entered the fight alongside al-Qaeda or the Taliban and (2) a co-belligerent with al-Qaeda or the Taliban in hostilities against the United States or its coalition partners. A group that embraces al-Qaeda's ideology without actually joining the fight alongside al-Qaeda is not an "associated force," nor is every group that commits or threatens to commit terrorist acts against U.S. persons an "associated force."

RESPONSE OF PROF. HAROLD HONGJU KOH TO QUESTION
SUBMITTED BY SENATOR BENJAMIN L. CARDIN

Administration officials have reported that U.S. reliance on war authorities undercuts our ability to cooperate with crucial partners and allies. In response to the 2011 deaths of two German citizens in Waziristan, Germany restricted information-sharing with the U.S. Further, Attorney General Eric Holder said "A number of countries have indicated that they will not cooperate with the United States in certain counterterrorism efforts if we intend to use that cooperation in pursuit of a military commission prosecution." The administration has also stated that Guantanamo, which is based on AUMF authority, "plagues our bilateral and multilateral relationships, creates friction with governments whose nationals we detain, provides cover for regimes whose detention practices we oppose, and provides our enemies with a symbol used to foster anti-U.S. sentiments around the world."

Question. How would a U.S. decision to expand or extend our use of war authorities to combat terrorism affect our global security cooperation?

Answer. As a former Legal Adviser and Assistant Secretary at the State Department, I am concerned that a U.S. decision to expand or extend our use of war authorities to combat terrorism could negatively affect our global security cooperation by undermining the trust and cooperation of critical allies. As I noted on page 14 of my written statement, "European courts are showing increased initiative in reviewing European cooperation in targeting operations for compliance with domestic and international law," which will likely have a chilling effect on multilateral cooperation. History suggests that concerns about legal liability may well reduce our allies' intelligence and security cooperation with the United States.

In the German example you cite, the claimants argued in a German federal court that Germany's transmission of data allegedly used to conduct a drone strike that resulted in the death of a German citizen abroad violated both international criminal law and the German criminal code.[1] Apparently, the threat of judicial review of drone strikes has already undermined intelligence-sharing with some key European allies who are worried about potential liability under their own domestic laws for cooperation. For example, in 2013, an anonymous British Government source told The New York Times that British intelligence agencies are increasingly concerned about the possibility of being "punished by the judiciary for something the Executive ordered them to do."[2] In 2013, British officials were sued by a Pakistani citizen of the United Kingdom whose father allegedly died in a U.S. drone strike abroad on a charge that they had unlawfully shared intelligence used to conduct the strike.[3] Although the Court of Appeal ultimately declined to hear the case based on the act of state doctrine, citing concerns that it would "necessarily entail a condemnation of the activities of the United States,"[4] British human rights groups condemned the dismissal and may well seek future litigation of similar cases.

European allies are also becoming concerned about potential liability under international law. In 2013, two human rights organizations filed a complaint with the International Criminal Court accusing several NATO member states, the United Kingdom, Germany, and Australia, of complicity in war crimes as a result of their alleged cooperation with American drone strikes abroad.[5] A Dutch NGO filed a similar lawsuit in November 2013, demanding that Dutch intelligence services stop using NSA data—which allegedly had not been obtained in accordance with Dutch law—to conduct drone strikes in Somalia, and expressed hope that the lawsuit would serve as a model for similar lawsuits challenging the legality of intelligence sharing with the United States.[6] Although the European Court of Human Rights has not considered the legality of targeted killing, in 2006, the Council of Europe asked the Venice Commission to review the application of the European Convention of Human Rights to collaborative intelligence activities. The resulting report asserted "member states have a strong duty to ensure that [the Convention] is respected by allied intelligence services operating within their own territory."[7] Recent history suggests that such issues introduce diplomatic tension with allies and reduce their intelligence and security cooperation out of concern for avoiding legal liability.[8]

End Notes

[1] See Louise Osborne, "Germany Denies Phone Data sent to NSA Used in Drone Attacks," The Guardian, Aug. 12, 2013.

[2] Ravi Somaiya, "Drone Strike Lawsuit Raises Concerns on Intelligence Sharing," N.Y. Times, Jan. 30, 2013.

[3] See *Noor Khan* v. *Secretary of State for Foreign and Commonwealth Affairs*, England and Wales Court of Appeal (Jan. 20, 2014).

[4] Shaheed Fatima, "Noor Khan: A Missed Opportunity?" Just Security (Jan. 30, 2014, 11:30 AM).

[5] Kevin Jon Heller, "The Reprieve Drone Strike Communication: Jurisdiction," Opinio Juris (Feb. 24, 2014, 3:55 PM).

[6] See New Europe Online, "Dutch Minister Faces NSA Lawsuit" (Jun. 11, 2013) (statement of lawyer for the coalition, that "[w]e based our case on European jurisdiction, so the case could simply be copied in other countries.").

[7] Richard J. Aldrich, "US-European Intelligence Co-operation on Counter-Terrorism: Low Politics and Compulsion," 11 Br. J. Polit. Int. Relat. 122, 133 (2009). Aldrich, a professor of international security at the University of Warwick who studies transatlantic intelligence cooperation, further noted that in recent years, Europeans are increasingly "looking over their shoulder at the provision of ECHR when working with the Americans whatever the location." Id. at 134.

[8] For example, in 2008, British officials demanded full details of intelligence-gathering flights the United States flew from a base in Cyprus, in case they "put the U.K. at risk of being complicit in unlawful acts." HMG Outlines New Procedures for Requesting Intel Flight Clearances (Apr. 18, 2008).